BERLITZ®

BERMUDA

1991/1992 Edition

By the staff of Berlitz Guides

How to use our guide

- All the practical information, hints and tips that you will need before and during the trip start on page 105.

- For general background, see the sections Bermuda and the Bermudians, p. 6, and A Brief History, p. 15.

- All the sights to see are listed between pages 27 and 85.
  ![Berlitz traveler symbol] Our own choice of sights most highly recommended is pinpointed by the Berlitz traveler symbol.

- Entertainment, nightlife and all other leisure activities are described between pages 85 and 99, while information on restaurants and cuisine is to be found on pages 100 to 104.

- Finally, there is an index at the back of the book, pp. 126–128.

Although we make every effort to ensure the accuracy of all the information in this book, changes occur incessantly. We cannot therefore take responsibility for facts, prices, addresses and circumstances in general that are constantly subject to alteration. Our guides are updated on a regular basis as we reprint, and we are always grateful to readers who let us know of any errors, changes or serious omissions they come across.

Text: Ken Bernstein
Photographer: Jürg Donatsch
Layout: Doris Haldemann
We wish to extend our warm thanks to the Bermuda Department of Tourism, and especially to Ann Minugh of the London office, for their help in the preparation of this guide. We're also very grateful to Charles Webbe, Manager of the Bermuda News Bureau.
Cartography: ● Falk-Verlag, Hamburg.

Contents

Maps

Cover picture: Jobson's Cove

Bermuda and the Bermudians

An outpost of beauty, tranquility and civility in mid-Atlantic, Bermuda beguiles visitors with its low-key charm. Helmeted "bobbies" in Bermuda shorts direct the traffic, which keeps to the left. The judges wear white wigs. At special ceremonies the governor steps out in full imperial regalia, plumed hat and all.

The name of the national game is cricket.

But the colony's British reserve sometimes yields to informality. The American connection goes back hundreds of years, so it's not surprising that hamburgers are as ubiquitous as fish and chips.

In terms of gross domestic product per capita, Bermuda counts as one of the world's ten richest countries. But despite all the wealth brought by tourism and high finance, and

the joys of the mild climate and pink beaches, the colony can't claim to have everything. Bermuda has no skyscrapers, parking meters or neon signs. It lacks pollution and slums. It doesn't even have income tax!

Bermuda, clearly, is a small wonder. With an area of about 20 square miles, it's slightly more confined than Manhattan Island, or the Channel island of Guernsey. (To put it into another perspective, Bermuda is 2,000 times smaller than Cuba.) So everything keeps to a modest scale, and you're always less than a mile from the ocean. Though it's actually possible to get lost, you only have to follow your nose to the nearest salt breeze.

Bermuda is not one island but a long, curving archipelago

Bermuda Supreme Court judges uphold British traditions; other less serious traditions (below).

of nearly 150. The seven principal islands are linked by causeways and bridges, including one that's proudly pointed out as the world's smallest drawbridge. All seven connected islands combine to give the impression of one lush body of land attended by throngs of picturesque islets and reefs.

Searchers for superlatives have determined that Bermuda is the world's "second most isolated island", outdone only by St. Helena, where Napoleon languished in exile. The nearest continental *terra firma* is Cape Hatteras, North Carolina, nearly 600 miles to the west.

Another distinction has been bestowed by geographers: just off Bermuda's shores may be found the most northerly coral reefs in the world. The coral—living organisms which multiply in colorful, fantastic shapes—provide the "floor show" for glass-bottomed boat excursions, which also feature a rainbow cast of playful fish. Snorkelers and scuba divers can mingle more intimately with these natural delights, but regulations imposed to preserve the coral reefs prohibit taking souvenirs of any kind.

Coral has played only a minor role in the evolution of Bermuda itself. The islands are founded on the peaks of an undersea range of volcanic mountains—but you needn't worry about eruptions or cataclysms, for the fire went out millions of years ago. Just beyond the reefs the ocean floor begins to plunge to a depth of three miles, but the shallow inner sea stays mostly calm, transparent and dreamily blue-green. As for the pink cast of the beaches, minute chips of sea shells and coral are scattered among the fine grains of sand.

Considering the beauty and fertility of the place, it's ironic that early navigators gave Bermuda such a wide berth. It had been on the map for nearly a century before the first colonists arrived, inadvertently, at the beginning of the 17th century. Sailors had long been uneasy about the Sargasso Sea, an area of the North Atlantic surrounding Bermuda, because of the profusion of seaweed which they feared might entangle their boats. They also worried about the sharp rocks and reefs encir-

Stately Camden House, official residence of Bermuda's premier, typifies the islands' architecture.

8

cling the islands. These obstacles wrecked many a ship, including the three-masted English flagship carrying the people who, as castaways, first settled here. The year was 1609. When the news reached England, it is thought to have inspired Shakespeare to write *The Tempest*, first performed in 1611.

Nowadays most visitors arrive by air, uneventfully but not without a certain feeling of drama. Flying over hundreds of miles of open ocean, it seems as if the navigator will never be able to locate a pinpoint of civilization in the middle of nowhere. The sudden sight of a sprawling group of green islands with white-roofed cottages ends the suspense with a sigh.

Mark Twain, who often visited Bermuda, described the roofs as "exactly the white of the icing on a cake". The effect can be blinding, but the color and the unique stepped shape are more than eye-catching architectural features. The roofs, which look like contour plans of snowcovered terraced mountains, channel rainwater into underground tanks. Bermuda needs all the water the sky provides, for there are no rivers or lakes.

Nor is there much spectacular scenery, aside from the beaches and the flaming sunsets. Don't expect any formidable cliffs or awesome mountain peaks. The island's high point is an unassuming 259 feet above sea level. The treats here are of a more modest nature: verdant gardens, pastel houses, sailboats scudding over an aquamarine sea, people who smile hello to strangers.

Like their forebears, who were sailors, fishermen, privateers and, frankly, pirates, the Bermudians are hardy and self-reliant. They respect the old traditions, the ceremonial occasions, the courtesies. With dignity and aplomb they wear Bermuda shorts (invented here, of course) along with ties and jackets, even on some very nippy winter days. They tend their gardens with British devotion, and name their pink, green or yellow houses something nautical or whimsical, like "On the Rocks", "Random Heights" or "Ada's Will Won". Instead of "hello" they may greet you with "all right", on the assumption you meant to ask, "How do you do?".

About six out of ten Bermudians are black. Their ancestors, in the main, were imported as slaves from the West Indies, about a thousand miles to the south. Emancipation came in 1834, three decades before the United States freed its slaves. Ties to the Caribbean remain: the sounds of calypso, steelband and reggae seem right at home in less-than-tropical Bermuda.

The most recent significant migration began in the 19th century, when farmers and gardeners arrived from the next group of islands east—the Azores. That strange nasal language you hear mumbled behind a flowering hedge is a mid-ocean version of Portuguese.

When the first English settlers arrived by chance, they were astonished to find a land of plenty. They could feast on wild pigs (descendants of some earlier castaways), giant turtles, birds so tame they flew into outstretched hands, and fish galore. It was too much of a good thing, and as early as 1620 Bermuda's first parliament felt obliged to pass a tortoise conservation act. Little of the early bounty survived all the gluttony except for the fish. Today about four-fifths of the food Bermudians and visitors consume must be imported.

The big agricultural export in the late 19th century was the Bermuda onion. But the word "Bermuda" couldn't be trade-marked and now most of the world's "Bermudas" are grown in Texas and California. The islands are still known as the Onion Patch and the inhabitants sometimes call themselves Onions. And they continue to grow the same mild, sweet Bermudas for local enjoyment—eaten solo, raw or baked, or contributing to almost any recipe. A member of the same botanical family, the Bermuda Easter Lily, constitutes the island's only big commercial crop, rushed to eager seasonal buyers in the U.S. and Canada.

Traditionally Bermuda's prevalent cedar trees were used for constructing ships and furniture, especially fragrant chests. But in the 1940s blight ravaged about 90 percent of them. Fast-growing casuarina or "whistling pine" have replaced much of the loss, though they haven't won the same place in the affections of the Bermudians. You'll also see palms, rubber trees and prolific citrus orchards. Bougainvillea, hibiscus, oleander and morning glory bloom in profusion along the narrow roads of Bermuda, and local gardeners coddle bird-of-paradise flowers, frangipani and orchids. Some estimates claim there are as many as 1,500 **11**

The day ends with a flourish on Hamilton Harbour and Great Sound.

species of trees, flowers and shrubs on the islands, from Acacia to Zygophyllaceae.

Meticulously groomed lawns surround the houses. In many countries grand villas are often hidden behind walls or dense foliage, but in Bermuda most of them are out in the open—not showing off, but not concealed from view either. And the houses obscured from land-

mingle with commuters on the small but serviceable local ferryboats.

The sea is the scene of the most varied activities. From the end of May to October the Atlantic is deemed most swimmable, though fanatics take to the alluring beaches at any time of the year; heated pools provide winter alternatives. Water sports enthusiasts go snorkeling, scuba diving and water skiing. The deep-sea, reef and shore fishing satisfy the best-traveled fishermen, the sort who know the difference between the tug of a tuna and a marlin. Boating for its own sake rounds out the ocean sports picture, with activities as heady as the classic Newport–Bermuda race, or as basic as trying out a rented Sunfish, or even a rowboat.

Of the landlocked sports, two rate special mention. Golf occupies a substantial portion of the island's real estate: seven 18-hole courses and several lesser establishments offer glorious ocean views, and challenge as well as charm. Tennis is played all around the islands, day and night, with a certain pride of seniority. In 1874, the game was introduced to the United States from Bermuda, where it was already popular.

ward passersby can usually be admired from sea or harborside.

Cruise-ship passengers get a good perspective of Bermuda—the lighthouses, hills and beaches, the country houses and picturesque townscapes. Sightseeing boats also cover the highlights. Or you can

13

About that time, visiting Bermuda first became fashionable, but far-off events kept interrupting the potential boom in tourism. First there was the Boer War, when P.O.W.s were corraled on the off-islands. World War I brought the submarine peril and fears of invasion. World War II had a more lasting effect, for the United States was given a sizable corner of Bermuda on which to build an airbase; the deal doesn't run out until the year 2040. Meanwhile passenger jets share the roomy runways with Navy patrol planes.

Some Bermudians and visitors will never forgive the Americans for introducing motor vehicles on the islands, hitherto traversed by bicycle and horse-and-buggy.

Cars were legalized in 1946, and the first little traffic jams soon developed. But most visitors still find the islands infinitely quieter and more relaxed than their home towns. And the occasional sound of a car horn is almost never a sign of alarm or annoyance. Typically, it's just Bermuda drivers greeting friends.

Waging a rear-guard action to cushion the impact of automobiles, the authorities permit only one to a family and forbid tourists to rent them. So the easiest and most amusing way for a visitor to explore the islands is to rent a moped, known locally as an "auxiliary cycle", and put-put from beach to historic fort to golf course to town. You can scoot from one end of Bermuda to the other in well under an hour and a half, but there's no rush, no reason not to take a spur-of-the-moment detour down Tribe Road No. 3 or Lovers Lane or any other byway you fancy. For more formal sightseeing there are bus tours; taxis flying a small blue flag are driven by qualified tour guides. For the romantic or nostalgic, fringed surreys make clip-clop excursions.

Other popular pursuits are browsing among the shops, carefully stocked with mainly British imports, and imbibing the atmosphere of the pubs. For such a small group of islands Bermuda manages to provide a big-time range of things to do, starting barefoot and working up to candlelit dinners in formal evening clothes. Whatever the magic, it lures more than 600,000 tourists a year—well over ten times the local population. And many of them return year after year. It's hard to beat a vacation in mid-ocean, at one remove from most of life's cares.

A Brief History

Columbus missed his chance. He was in the area in 1492, but in his westward rush to find the riches of the East he failed to discover Bermuda. The credit goes instead to a Spanish navigator, Juan Bermúdez, after whom the place was named. He took note of the islands in 1503, and only eight years later they were shown on an Italian map as "La Bermuda". Early navigators called them the "Isles of Devils". They were terrified of Bermuda's reefs and celebrated their salvation when they had passed safely by. One who didn't make it was the anonymous sailor who carved the date 1543 on a rock on the south coast, now known as Spanish Rock. He also inscribed a cross and a pair of letters, perhaps his initials or those of his king, but they can't quite be deciphered.

The first Englishman to set foot on Bermuda was a sailor named Henry May, working on a French ship which foundered on the northern reefs in 1593. The crew built a getaway boat and succeeded in return-

Bermuda in a Nutshell

Geography: Bermuda is an archipelago of some 150 islands and islets in the North Atlantic, 600 miles east of Cape Hatteras, North Carolina. Land area is about 20 square miles.

Population: 57,000, of whom more than 60 percent are black.

Government: Bermuda is a self-governing British colony headed by a governor representing the Crown, a premier and cabinet appointed by the governor, with an appointed Senate and an elected House of Assembly (parliament).

Economy: Tourism, by far the biggest industry, generates most of Bermuda's foreign exchange earnings. Another major economic factor: international "exempted" companies using Bermuda as a base for "offshore" operations. Of the national budget, 20 percent goes for education, and less than 2 percent for defense.

Religion: Protestants make up the majority of the population, with Anglicans the largest denomination.

Language: English

ing to Europe. Ten years later a Spanish galleon accidentally visited Bermuda and the crew lived to tell the tale. But eye-witness reports of this small group of islands well endowed with fish, birds, tortoises and wild pigs set off no stampede of settlers. Despite benign conditions, the "Isles of Devils" kept their reputation as a treacherous obstruction between the West Indies and Europe. What the land speculators really coveted was the American continent.

Sea Venture

In 1606 James I granted a charter to the Virginia Company to establish the first English colony in America, obligingly named Jamestown in the king's honor. Three years later a second contingent of settlers set sail from Plymouth under Admiral Sir George Somers. The trip was a disaster.

Less than halfway across the Atlantic the fleet ran into a vicious storm. The flagship, a 300-ton vessel called *Sea Venture*, was detached from the rest of the convoy, only to be engulfed by a hurricane. The leaking ship, with 150 people aboard, snagged on the reefs just east of Bermuda on July 28, 1609. Miraculously, all aboard were ferried to shore.

It turned out that Bermuda was an ideal place to be stranded. The islands were abundantly supplied with food, semi-tropically comfortable, and devoid of deadly animals —or dangerous natives who might object to sharing the wealth. A less ambitious group leader might have scrapped the uncertain Virginia project and settled down to beach-combing in Bermuda. But not Sir George Somers.

He rallied his pioneers to build escape ships from local cedar and timber salvaged from the remains of the *Sea Venture*. Leaving behind only two men—deserters—the Somers party resumed the journey westward. Just short of a year after the expedition had left England, they finally landed at Jamestown, to be greeted by a shocking letdown. Indian massacres, illness and simple starvation had decimated the colony.

In light of the tragedy, Admiral Somers changed his opinion of Bermuda. It could provide the people of Jamestown with enough food to save them from further hardship. So he sailed back to the erstwhile "Isles of Devils" to set up a relief program. But it was all too much for the gallant admiral, who died trying to organize the Bermuda-James-town lifeline. His body was shipped back to England but his heart was buried in Bermuda, the colony he founded just by chance.

London eventually saw the value of a mid-ocean base at Bermuda. In the spring of 1612 more than 50 colonists were sent out to join three pioneers who had volunteered to hold the fort. With this population boom, defenses were built and a town established—St. George's, at the east end of Bermuda, near the spot where the *Sea Venture* castaways had first landed.

News of the expanding British settlement agitated the Spanish court. After all, a Spaniard had discovered (and given his name to) Bermuda; other Spaniards had spent time there. And now King Philip III squirmed as the palace "hawks" urged him to oust the English "pirates" by force. With characteristic vagueness, the king compromised on a low-budget reconnaissance mission before making any decisions. Two small Spanish ships were sent out to reconnoiter Bermuda. As they approached, they were met by two quick salvos from a cannon fired, as it happened, by the governor him-

The Deliverance *ferried ship-wrecked colonists to Jamestown.*

self. Grossly overestimating the strength of the English garrison, which couldn't have mustered a third shot at that time, the Spaniards fled. Bermuda's Britishness was affirmed. **17**

A Growing Colony

In the first few years of the colony's existence progress was swift. A society, not just a fortress, was being established.

In 1619 the congregation of St. Peter's church moved into a permanent building. Bermuda's parliament met in an enclosure still visible amid the pews of St. Peter's, the oldest Anglican church in continuous use in the western hemisphere. But it was soon decided to distance the secular from the religious and a separate government building went up. State House, Bermuda's first stone structure, still stands.

An English surveyor, Richard Norwood, undertook a monumental study of the terrain, dividing the colony into "tribes", which are the parishes (counties) of today. Special Bermuda money was minted, with a sailing ship on one side and a wild pig on the other, hence the name "hog money". These coins, extremely rare and valuable today, were Britain's first colonial currency. The present-day Bermuda pennies have a commemorative pig on the reverse but are worth only one cent.

Agriculture was to be the economic base for the new colony. However, it didn't work very well in practice. The first major crop was tobacco but somehow Bermuda leaf never enjoyed as much success as the crop from Virginia.

A side-effect of agricultural development was the introduction of slaves from the West Indies. Almost from the colony's foundation its bi-racial future was foreshadowed. Ber-

mudians maintain that the slaves were well treated, in part because the impersonal plantation system never existed. (By 1834, when slavery was abolished in British possessions, blacks made up the majority of Bermuda's population.)

Turning to the all-encompassing sea, Bermuda went into the whaling business. This made sense, for the islands stand astride the main whale migration route, and England

Although the neat paintwork of St. Peter's belies its age, Bermuda's oldest church dates from 1619.

paid well for the oil. Once the colonists were good enough seamen to land whales, it was perhaps inevitable that they should turn to piracy. The practice evolved modestly, perhaps even legally, from wrecking—the salvage of treasure found on ships grounded on the local reefs. From there it was easy to make the transition to privateering (a semantic nicety) or piracy on the high seas. Smuggling was so commonplace it passed almost unnoticed.

In the late 17th century the islanders' search for a livelihood went to amazing lengths. The colony developed its own satellite nearly a thousand miles to the south. The uninhabited, sandy Turks Islands, half the size of the Bermuda group, were so hot and dry they proved ideal for the production of salt from the sea. Bermudians practically commuted to the Turks to rake the salt ponds every summer, stopping in American ports on the way home to trade the salt for food. For more than a century it was the only kind of "farming" at which Bermudians excelled. But in 1799 the Turks fell under the jurisdiction of the Bahamas and Bermuda's salty enterprise in mini-imperialism came to an end.

Changing Loyalties

Isolated from London by more than 3,300 miles in an age of slow and chancy communications, Bermuda sometimes found itself out of step with developments in the motherland. In 1649 the islanders were appalled to learn of the execution of King Charles I and the proclamation of Cromwell's Commonwealth. Bermuda resisted the Puritan regime until the Long Parliament banned all trade with the colony, considered to be in a state of insurrection. Cromwellian rules soon reigned in Bermuda, and among other rigors a series of witchcraft purges ensued. In all, five of the accused were put to death. As for Bermuda's royalists, they rejoiced in 1660 when Charles II was restored to the throne.

Another era ended in 1684 when the Bermuda Company lost its charter. Until then the colony had been administered privately, having been founded, like Virginia, as a commercial venture. After a five-year legal battle, Bermuda became a British colony with a degree of self-government. The last governor representing the company was reappointed by the Crown. He was Colonel Richard Coney, after whom it is believed Bermuda's Coney Island was named.

One of Bermuda's greatest governors was Alured (an archaic form of Alfred) Popple, an intellectual aristocrat who took office in 1738. He introduced some scientific and technological novelties to the islands—a microscope, a telescope, his personal collection of a thousand books, and a sedan-chair, which inspired a new mode of travel on the narrow, hilly streets of St. George's. When Popple died in 1744 of a "bilious fever", the islanders erected a plaque you can still read in St. Peter's Church. The inscription extols at notable length the virtues of the "Good Governor", such as elegance, simplicity, hospitality and benevolence.

The most difficult test of Bermuda's loyalties came when the American colonies rose in rebellion against George III. London forbade Bermuda to trade with or otherwise support General Washington's revolutionaries, a heartbreaking decree for the islanders to obey. Bermuda had always maintained close personal ties with the people of Virginia and other American colonies; commercial considerations also provided a strong rationale for helping the rebels. Simply put, Bermuda needed food and George Washington needed gunpowder.

To the horror of the British colonial authorities, a daring and highly irregular bargain was struck. Persons unknown —to this day—broke into an ammunition magazine in St. George's on a night in mid-August 1775. They filched 100 kegs of gunpowder and rolled them down the hill to Tobacco Bay to be ferried to an American frigate standing by beyond the reefs.

George Washington hadn't heard about the gunpowder caper three weeks after the fact, when he wrote a letter to "the inhabitants of the Islands of Bermuda". After four wordy paragraphs of niceties, the general got down to business: "We are informed there is a very large magazine on your island under a very feeble guard... We know not... to what extent to solicit your assistance in availing ourselves of this supply...." The letter was never delivered, for the gunpowder had already been "liberated" for rebel use.

Later in the Revolutionary War, Bermudians were given the opportunity to strike a few blows for the Crown. Bermuda privateers captured dozens of American ships.

Bard of Bermuda

The Royal Navy buildup accounted for the islands' proudest literary connection. In 1803 a young Irish-born poet and composer, Thomas Moore, was sent to Bermuda as Registrar to the Court of Vice-Admiralty. Among other poems he wrote during three-and-a-half months here was an ode to "the little fairy isle", which he called

> ... a heaven for love to sigh in,
> For bards to live and saints
> to die in.

Tom Moore (1779–1852), a friend of Byron and Shelley, is best known for the songs, *The Last Rose of Summer* and *Believe Me If All Those Endearing Young Charms*. He made poetry a profitable profession. A London publisher paid him £3,000 for the poem *Lalla Rookh*—before he had written a line.

Gibraltar of the West

With the loss of its naval bases in the American colonies, Britain began to appreciate Bermuda's potential as a strategic asset. The sequel to the Revolutionary War, the War of 1812, proved the island's value as the Royal Navy's "Gibraltar of the West". From here the king's men-of-war sailed to battle, often returning with captured American vessels.

Local privateers conducted a parallel effort with some success.

A big new dockyard took shape on Ireland Island, at the opposite end of the archipelago from the population center of St. George's. With this shift in the center of gravity, the capital was transferred in 1815 from St. George's to the hitherto undistinguished village of Hamilton. Traditionalists were furious.

To supplement the slave labor working on the dockyard project, Britain sent convicts to Bermuda, starting in 1824. At any time well over 1,000 prisoners were employed in the development of the outpost's military potential. Yellow fever, dysentery and scurvy killed a sizeable proportion of these unfortunates, who were crammed into filthy floating prisons during the hours they weren't working.

Pressure for abolition of the hulks, or at least better working conditions, came from many quarters, including Bermuda's Governor Charles Elliot. He had already made his mark as Britain's chief administrator in China, where he was credited with acquiring Hong Kong for the Crown. He had also enjoyed the distinction of being British Chargé d'Affaires to the Republic of Texas in the early 1840s. But his efforts to stamp out the indignity of the hulks went nowhere, and these relics of a cruel age were not abandoned until 1863.

American Civil War

Slavery had been abolished in Bermuda more than a quarter-century before the outbreak of the American Civil War, yet islanders' sympathies lay with the South. One reason was the traditional and family link with Virginia and nearby states. Another was the commercial angle: blockade-running could be fabulously lucrative. Even though British subjects were specifically forbidden from taking part in the hostilities in any way, Bermudians pitched in to help the Confederacy survive. Feelings

Neptune figurehead symbolizes Bermuda's seafaring traditions.

ran so high that the islanders ostracized and even physically harrassed the American Consul, who represented the Lincoln government.

Bermuda served as a handy supply base for the Confederacy. Steamships from Europe laden with food or arms waited their turn in St. George's Harbour to unload cargoes which were then transferred onto blockade-runners. These long, slim vessels, which burned smokeless fuel to decrease the risk of detection, were specially designed to outrun Yankee picket ships. Arriving at a Southern port, they would take on a new cargo of cotton—a most profitable ballast which increased in value tenfold by the time it was delivered to buyers in Britain. St. George's boomed during the Civil War; the town seethed with sailors, speculators, Confederate procurement agents and Union spies. When General Lee laid down his sword in 1865 it was as if Bermuda, too, had lost a war.

Three More Wars
At the turn of the century the Boer War, the struggle between British and Dutch settlers in South Africa, sent shock waves as far as Bermuda. Thousands of Boer prisoners were shipped to the colony and P.O.W. camps were established on half a dozen islands in Great Sound. When the Boers lost the war in 1900 most of the prisoners accepted the verdict, swore allegiance to Britain and were repatriated. But an unreconciled few never left Bermuda. For years these veterans with long beards lingered on as familiar local characters, living by the sale of their woodcarvings.

During World War I, Bermudian volunteers fought in France, while others joined resident British forces in defending the islands. German submarines aggravated the supply problem and threatened the ships which stopped at the islands to refuel for the remainder of the Atlantic crossing. When the United States entered the conflict, White's Island, just opposite the Hamilton waterfront, was leased to the U.S. government as a base for sub-chasers. It was a small-scale preview of the American military presence which would be established in Bermuda in World War II.

Between the wars tourism became a major economic factor. Luxury cruise liners began regular runs between New

York and Bermuda during the Roaring Twenties. Resort hotels were built to attract Americans escaping the northern winter—and the inconvenience of the Prohibition laws.

When war broke out in Europe in 1939 Bermuda's young tourist industry all but collapsed. Nobody was interested in luxury cruises through submarine-infested seas to a blacked-out island where food was rationed. Anyway, the ships were being converted to troop transports. Some of the big hotels served as posh billets for servicemen and civilian war workers.

The most intriguing aspect of Bermuda's World War II role wasn't revealed until long afterward. In the basements of the Princess and Bermudiana hotels, more than a thousand British experts analyzed communications intercepted between the western hemisphere and Europe. Mail quietly removed from refuelling ships and planes was steamed open and tested for microdots and invisible codes, an important contribution to the struggle against Axis espionage.

Just as the first MI5 ferrets were arriving in Hamilton in August, 1940, the "lend-lease" agreement between Britain and the United States was announced. Under a 99-year lease the U.S. acquired about one-tenth of the land area of Bermuda for the development of naval and air bases. While Bermudians served at the war fronts with British forces (still segregated into white and colored battalions), Allied engineers extended and modernized the defenses of Britain's "Gibraltar of the West".

Changing Times

After the war, a centuries-old link with Britain was cut. As the empire contracted, British military forces were pulled out of Bermuda. Domestically, social changes shook the old way of life, starting with the introduction of cars, which captured the previously peaceful roads.

In 1959 racial segregation ended in the major hotels and restaurants, but schools were not integrated until 1971. Women's suffrage had been achieved in 1944; in 1963 the old law restricting the vote to landowners was tossed aside. Five years later a new constitution was adopted to make island self-government more representative and effective. And then in 1970 the colony was expelled from the Sterling area, forcing Bermuda to hitch its currency to the U.S. dollar. **25**

During this era of rapid change the strains on Bermudians showed. Riots broke out in 1968 and British troops had to be called in to restore order. Five years later the governor, Sir Richard Sharples, and his aide were assassinated. The motive could never be established, but when the alleged assassins were executed in 1977 more riots rocked Bermuda.

In the 1970s the island was featured in a rash of articles

Bermuda's affable bobbies are in themselves a tourist attraction.

and books devoted to a "phenomenon" dubbed the Bermuda Triangle. These were based on reports of planes and ships which had vanished in the area, and spiced with hints of supernatural and extraterrestrial forces. Sceptics point out that similar mysteries occur in other parts of the world, but the rewrite men happened to find the one-time "Isles of Devils" a glamorous setting.

Bermudians were more concerned with another long-standing nautical phenomenon: cargo ships supplying Bermuda's needs depart with empty holds, for the colony produces no tangible exports. The only solution has been to increase the income earned from tourism, insurance and banking enterprises. In the seventies the number of so-called exempt companies based in Bermuda more than doubled. These firms, attracted by tax advantages and flawless communications, contribute to the balance of payments surplus almost half the amount of revenue earned by tourism.

But prosperity can't solve all the problems. There's a need for improved racial harmony; and inflation, as almost everywhere, is a burden. The influx of foreign executives and technicians has put severe pressure on the housing supply. And there remains a fundamental issue Bermuda will have to face: what role can a colony play in the post-colonial era? Will Bermuda's future point instead toward independence? The grave debate stirs high feelings. But history indicates that Bermuda, as ever, will be equal to the challenge.

What to See

Whether you arrive by air or sea, your first close look at Bermuda will focus on the easternmost islands. Airliners land at the U.S. Naval Air Station on St. David's Island. Ships pick up a pilot off St. George's Island, continuing into historic St. George's Harbour or taking the long way around to Hamilton Harbour.

Organized excursions to the islands' historic and scenic highspots by bus or taxi can start anywhere—from the waterfront at Hamilton or St. George's or from the resort hotels, scattered over all nine parishes. A variety of boat tours are available, and restful roaming by horse-and-carriage starts at the quaysides. Many visitors rent mopeds for improvised sightseeing. Shorter-range excursions on rented pedal bikes or afoot can be combined with ferryboat trips. And the public bus system goes within easy distance of all the principal attractions.

We've elected to begin our survey of Bermuda with Hamilton, the colony's capital, and then to work our way from the center of population and commerce to the extremities of the archipelago.

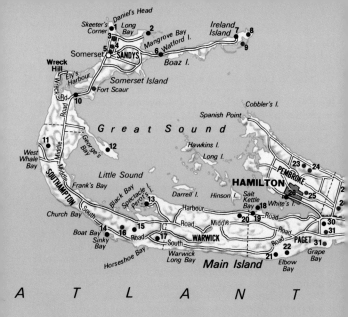

1 Canadian Forces Station Bermuda

2 Cambridge Beaches Hotel

3 Springfield

4 Gilbert Nature Reserve

5 St. James's Church

6 Watford Bridge

7 Casemate Prison

8 Dockyard

9 Maritime Museum & Keepyard

10 Somerset Bridge

11 Port Royal Golf Course

12 U. S. Naval Air Station Annex

13 Riddell's Bay Golf & Country Club

14 Sonesta Beach Hotel

15 Southampton Princess Hotel

16 Gibbs Hill Lighthouse

17 Warwick Camp

18 Glencoe Hotel

19 Inverurie Hotel

20 Belmont Hotel

21 Elbow Beach Hotel

22 Stonington Beach Hotel

23 Black Watch Well

24 Government House

25 Fort Hamilton

26 Ferry Station

27 Ocean View Golf & Country Club

28 Arboretum

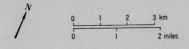

BERMUDA

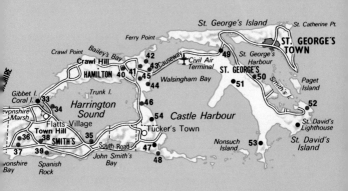

29 Old Devonshire Church
30 King Edward VII Memorial Hospital
31 Bermuda Botanical Gardens
32 Palm Grove Garden
33 Flatts Inlet
34 Bermuda Aquarium
35 Devil's Hole
36 Verdmont
37 St. Patrick's Roman Catholic Church
38 St. Mark's Church
39 Spittal Pond Nature Reserve
40 Bermuda Museum
41 Perfume Factory
42 Grotto Bay Beach & Tennis Club

43 Bermuda Pottery
44 Blue Hole Grotto (Dolphin Show)
45 Crystal Caves
46 Leamington Caves
47 Mid-Ocean Club
48 Natural Arches
49 Swing Bridge
50 Carter House
51 U. S. Naval Air Station
52 Great Head Park
53 N. A. S. A. Tracking Station
54 Castle Harbour Hotel

Hamilton

When the cruise ships dock opposite the quaint buildings of Front Street they tower over the town, making it seem as if Hamilton is tied up to the ships and not the other way around. And these are only the smaller cruise ships; massive liners have to weigh anchor in Great Sound and ferry their passengers to town aboard launches.

The city of Hamilton fills an area of less than half a square mile. The population numbers only about 3,000, but the surrounding parish of Pembroke adds another 10,000 to the "metropolitan" total.

Founded in 1793, Hamilton is an architectural medley of old, low-lying wooden and limestone buildings, often adorned with decorative arcades or balconies, and tidy white-roofed cottages and homesteads. Among these have sprung up modern new office buildings which some critics decry as irrelevant (and irreverent) to Bermuda's architectural heritage. But in the profusion of semitropical greenery, it all fits together rather pain-

At dockside or in Perot Post Office, Hamilton charms visitors.

lessly. And the proximity of the harbor, bustling with yachts, liners, freighters and ferries, adds fascination to the scene.

A likely place to start any visit to Hamilton is the **Visitors Service Bureau** on the waterfront, operated by the Chamber of Commerce. Free maps, literature and advice are available. A few steps away is the **Ferry Terminal,** headquarters of the colony's heavily subsidized harbor transportation system. Before the age of the ferry, rowboats provided a shortcut to the opposite shore, a service which endured until 1950.

At the intersection of Queen and Front streets stands what is probably Bermuda's most photographed landmark, although it's only 20 years old and of limited aesthetic merit. This is the **Birdcage,** a shaded platform for a policeman supervising the traffic at this difficult junction. Like the guardsmen at Buckingham Palace, the constables who draw this assignment are accustomed to being gawked at and asked to pose, and they keep their good humor throughout.

Queen Street, running inland from the harborfront here, provides a microcosm of Bermuda in its couple of hun-

dred yards: historic buildings, exotic flora, shops for tourists and locals, an Olde English pub and an American-style fast-food emporium.

Electric light bulbs simulating the flicker and obscurity of 19th-century lamps add to the atmosphere inside the **Perot Post Office,** a nicely restored white house with big black shutters. This is a working branch post office with a distinguished postmark. Here in 1848 Bermuda's Postmaster William B. Perot issued and signed the colony's first postage stamps, which are now considered exquisite rarities of the philatelic world. This is a convenient and appropriate place to buy stamps for your postcards.

Perot lived in the handsome homestead behind the post office, now occupied by the **Bermuda Library** and the Historical Society's Museum. The colossal rubber tree shading the lawn arrived from British Guyana in 1847; its rampaging roots are said to reach to the seafront. The library boasts a bumper collection of Bermudiana and a useful general reference department; on the floor above is a general circulating library with reading rooms and facilities for listening to music.

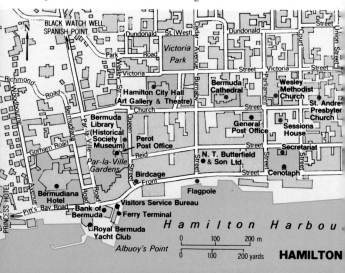

Sharing the ground floor with the library, the **Bermuda Historical Society Museum** preserves unusual curios from the island's past. The exhibits ought to interest history buffs, antiquarians and coin collectors. There are models of the ships first used in the colony and copies of the earliest maps of Bermuda. Note the fine old silverware crafted by island artisans and classic cedar tables and chairs.

Par-la-Ville Gardens, which surrounds the library and museum building, was the Perot family's property. Now it's a well-kept public park with shade trees and beds of bright blooming flowers.

Queen Street climbs as far as Church Street, a main east-west thoroughfare named for its heavy incidence of churches. The most spectacular building here is the modern **Hamilton City Hall,** opened in 1960. Most Bermuda buildings have gleaming white roofs, but the walls of this one are whitewashed, too. The elegant tower is topped by a weathervane in the form of a model of the sailing ship *Sea Venture*, ground-

The mini-motorbike brigade meets up at Hamilton's trim City Hall.

ed off Bermuda in 1609. What at first glance looks like the municipal clock is actually a wind direction gauge, the pointer controlled by the little ship above.

The interior of City Hall contains a bold, high-ceilinged reception hall, an art gallery, exhibition hall and a comfortable theater. City Hall was built on the site of the Hamilton Hotel, a sprawling landmark begun in the 1850s, when only the most visionary Bermudians could have believed in the potential of tourism. During World War II the hotel was converted to government use, and it burned down in 1955 in spite of the best efforts of the islands' fire fighters, civilian and military.

Across Victoria Street from the rear of City Hall lies Victoria Park, an agreeable patch of green with a bandstand in the middle, built in honor of Queen Victoria's jubilee. Bermuda has many monuments, but for hazy reasons of its own the colony erects no statues honoring historic figures. Not even Queen Victoria rates an effigy in stone or bronze in this park which bears her name— or anywhere else on the statueless islands.

The tallest tower on Hamilton's skyline belongs to the Anglican **Bermuda Cathedral,** officially the Cathedral of the Most Holy Trinity. The first church on this site was burnt down in 1884 by an arsonist so broadminded in his grudges that he also set fire to the Catholic church and some non-denominational buildings as well. The new cathedral, consecrated in 1911, follows the Early English style. If it weren't for the row of majestic palms alongside, it could be a church almost anywhere in Britain. While the church was under construction a hurricane hit Bermuda, giving the architect second thoughts about the potential strains on his building; he decided that security should take precedence over mere aesthetics, which explains the eight extra columns reinforcing the main piers. Problems with the weather also account for mismatched colors in the stonework around the exterior of windows and doors. The original stone from Normandy began to crumble under the influence of Bermuda's salt air and required wholesale replacement. Other stone used in the project—from

Bermuda's cathedral of 1911 perpetuates the Early English style.

Nova Scotia, Indiana and Bermuda itself—has borne up well under local conditions.

Two more major churches farther east on Church Street are also fixtures from the Victorian era: Wesley Methodist Church and St. Andrew's Presbyterian Church.

The solid white modern building at the corner of Church and Parliament streets is the nerve center of Bermuda's postal service. Among the departments of the General

Quality goods at advantageous prices lure shoppers to Bermuda.

Post Office is a philatelic bureau with mint sheets of the latest issues as well as a supply of back issues of Bermuda stamps. If you just want to send your postcards, the ordinary service windows in the G.P.O. sell colorful stamps without all the fuss and mystique the collectors enjoy.

You may wonder about the pink Italianate clock tower attached to the momentous arcaded building that stands in its own hilltop park across Parliament Street. The tower was an afterthought of 1887, designed to enhance the pretensions of what began as a fairly austere early 19th-century structure. This is **Sessions House,** headquarters of two elements of Bermuda's goverment. The upper floor belongs to the Assembly, where local M.P.s debate the issues of the day in a stately wood-panelled chamber. As in the Mother of Parliaments in London the Speaker, white-wigged and black-gowned, looks down at rows of members facing each other as Government and Opposition. But the Bermuda M.P.s have the advantage of comfortable armchairs and desks. If the parliamentary debate is too arcane or long-winded you might look in on the Bermuda Supreme Court, which holds forth on the ground floor. Here, too, wigs and gowns are the uniform for the judge and the barristers. "Respectable" dress is required of the public.

Down the hill, the classical **Cabinet Building** or Secretariat enjoys a spacious landscaped setting. The upper house of **37** the legislature, the appointed Senate, holds its meetings here, as do the premier and his cabinet. In this two-story Bermuda limestone building, completed in 1836, sessions of Parliament are inaugurated with elaborate ceremonial color, reminiscent of equivalent rituals at Westminster. The annual ceremony, in mid-October, starts with a formal parade by the redcoats of the Bermuda Regiment. Then the governor arrives, wearing a uniform that might have been borrowed from Gilbert and Sullivan, topped by an ostrich-plumed hat. He inspects the spit-and-polish honor guard before being invited inside to deliver his "Speech from the Throne" outlining government policies.

Facing Front Street, the Cenotaph honors the dead of two world wars. It's a scaled-down copy of the war memorial in London's Whitehall.

Front Street, dividing the town from the harborfront, has the air of an exotic trading port. And well it might; one strong motive for moving the colonial capital to Hamilton in 1815 was to keep a closer eye on all the smuggling. The 18th and 19th-century buildings of Front Street, with their arcades, verandas and filigree, have survived many a drama. The shops within specialize in Bermuda's best-known contemporary imports—tweeds, cashmere, crystal and china from the Old Country.

The Union Jack flying at the foot of Burnaby Street marks a spot known simply as the Flagpole. In the days before radio, this was the place seamen looked for storm warnings. If you listen to Bermuda's commercial radio stations today you may be startled to hear this announcement: "Fish for sale at the Flagpole!". It means one of the local fishing boats has arrived at the dock below the flagpole, and the captain and mate are chopping the big ones into steaks.

Front Street also accommodates the offices of airlines and travel agencies and the headquarters of Bermuda's two biggest banks. The highly developed banking system, armed with expertise in international dealings and the benefits of instant satellite communications, helps to account for the colony's success as an important offshore business center.

On the landward side, the Bank of N.T. Butterfield & Son Limited, Bermuda's oldest bank, occupies a solid, porticoed building, traditional in style but computerized within.

Down the road on the opposite side, the Bank of Bermuda Limited operates from a new seven-story building which almost qualifies as a skyscraper in these low-lying surroundings. On the mezzanine floor you can see the bank's precious **Coin Exhibition,** which starts with rare examples of hog money, Bermuda's first crude coins. It goes on to display one of each British coin minted since the islands were settled, and there are additional scores of coins tracing the development of currency in the western hemisphere. An illustrated guidebook to this most comprehensive collec-

Front Street's shady arcades line the Hamilton harborfront.

tion, available without charge at the bank, makes fascinating reading for anyone interested in numismatics or history.

Between the bank and the harbor is a little peninsula called Albuoy's Point, which contains a small, well-tended park. From here you can catch a glimpse of the privileged world of the **Royal Bermuda Yacht Club,** whose quaint pink headquarters building is next door. The club, organized in 1844, sponsors the elite Newport–Bermuda Ocean Yacht **39**

Race every other year. But in any season you'll find dreamy yachts, local and from faraway ports, tied up at the club's docks.

At least once a month from April through September, Front Street is the setting for one of Bermuda's most ceremonial occasions, **Beating Retreat.** Members of the Bermuda Regiment in their red and gold full-dress uniforms march to bagpipes and drums, recreating the 16th-century ritual of mounting the night watch. The pipers, of course, wear kilts.

On an ordinary day on Front Street the costumes are more what you're accustomed to, except for the proliferation of Bermuda shorts, the policemen in their Scotland Yard helmets and the traffic wardens snooping among the parked cars in yellow-tabbed black uniforms identical to those of their counterparts in London. Some surrey drivers wear pith helmets.

From a lavishly landscaped eminence at the west end of the city, the **Bermudiana Hotel** surveys the harbor. The Furness Withy shipping line founded the hotel in the 1920s to cater to the visitors its luxury liners were beginning to bring to the island. The six-story resort hotel burned down in 1958 but was soon rebuilt.

The only other major hotel within walking distance of Hamilton, the **Princess,** is farther west along the waterfront road, whose name changes here to Pitts Bay Road. The Princess, a century-old institution, has expanded into a vast, modern complex with its own dock for yachts, sightseeing boats and deep-sea fishing craft. The hotel's name was inspired by the visit there in 1883 of Princess Louise, Queen Victoria's daughter. During World War II British counter-intelligence specialists intercepted and censored international communications in the hotel basements.

The Outskirts of Hamilton

The rest of Pembroke parish, which surrounds Hamilton, is too far-flung to be seen on foot. If you follow Pitts Bay Road by taxi or bike all the way to its western extremity, you wind up at **Spanish Point.** This is believed to be the spot where a shipwrecked Spanish crew spent three weeks of 1603 repairing their galleon before resuming the journey to Spain. This preceded the arrival of the first British settlers, a chronological detail which caused some Spanish resentment once

Bermuda's strategic importance became obvious. Today, in spite of the sandy beach and the pleasant sight of boats bobbing at anchor, the bay has the air of an isolated Pacific atoll. The ugly remains of what 19th-century engineers hailed as the world's largest floating dockyard now protect the little harbor from heavy tides. The wreck was being towed away for scrap in 1902 when it ran aground here.

Half a mile to the east is another of the more than 30 public beaches round the islands. It's part of Admiralty House Park, which was the official residence of the Royal Navy's regional commander until 1956.

Another military echo along North Shore Road: Black Watch Well, marked with a memorial tablet, was dug by troops of that Scottish regiment during a drought in 1849.

A variation on the Union Jack, with Bermuda's coat of arms in the center, flies over **Government House** on a hill with views of the ocean to the north and the city of Hamilton to the south. The Victorian mansion is a curious collection

Ever loyal to Queen and country, the regimental band plays on.

of architectural quirks, from broad verandas to stubby towers. The immensity of the house fits into the lush vastness of semitropical gardens. Queen Elizabeth II, Sir Winston Churchill, John F. Kennedy and many other notables have been guests at Government House, but it's closed to the public.

You don't need an invitation from the governor or even the mayor to enjoy the sensational **view** over Hamilton and its harbor from the heights of **Fort Hamilton.** This Victorian fort, on a strategic hilltop at the east end of the city, is open for inspection all day. It's also a fine spot for relaxation, with grassy knolls covering most of the menacing military construction. But several huge old cannon peek over the ramparts as a reminder of the defensive purpose for which the fort was built in 1889. Actually, the cannon—ten-inchers which fired 400-pound shells—were moved here from another Bermuda fort for a bit of added atmosphere. Among other attractions is the labyrinth of underground passages.

For old and young, fat and thin, Bermuda shorts are de rigueur.

South and West from Hamilton

Paget is the parish (county) across the harbor from the city of Hamilton. To get there you can take the ferry or follow the road, named Crow Lane, looping around the inner harbor. The very innermost stretch of the harbor is protected by a thick mangrove patch known as DUCK ISLAND, behind which ducks and small boats shelter in stormy weather. The ducks also enjoy taking the sun on the grass of the tiny Foot-of-Crow-Lane Park.

The road intersection here is in the form of a roundabout (traffic circle). If you're riding a bike, be alert to the local rules: yield to any traffic already in the circle before you enter, and don't forget that traffic moves clockwise. Note that Bermuda's road signs give distances in **kilometers, not miles** (1 km = .621 mile).

Point Finger Road, parallel to the main road south from the roundabout, seems to have been named after an old-fashioned sign that once indicated its direction. The imposing building on the east side set back amid towering palm trees is the 300-bed King Edward VII Memorial Hospital.

The hospital's fine trees and gardens come with the compliments of its next-door neighbor, the **Botanical Gardens.** This 36-acre park makes a good starting point for a study of the islands' flowers and trees, as well as of some outlandish species imported from distant climes. Guided tours set out from the main parking lot; there are good maps for independent tours of the gardens.

Wherever you roam in the Botanical Gardens you'll marvel at nature's variety, admirable or grotesque: the delicate, almost microscopic flowers growing from cactus plants, the broad palette of colors of hibiscus, the Tarzanesque vines of monstrous banyan trees, the long and the short of the palm family.

For Bermuda's Department of Agriculture and Fisheries, which runs the gardens, it's a matter of business and pleasure. Botanical experiments are always underway, and there are frequent special events—the annual Agricultural Exhibition, the Poultry Show and Citrus Exhibition, and horse, dog and bird shows.

On the grounds of the Botanical Gardens, a classic Bermuda house with verandas on two stories, rather like an old Southern mansion, has been meticulously restored. **Camden House** is noted for the cedar carvings and panelling within and the stately lawn with views out over the sea. The Bermuda government has made Camden an official residence for the premier, after the manner of the Chequers estate in Britain, a country refuge for the incumbent of No. 10 Downing Street.

Along the North Coast

Heading west from that main traffic circle, Harbour Road covers the north coast of Paget and Warwick parishes, an area of luxuriant vegetation and luxurious villas. The **view** across the water to Hamilton is a charmer, too. The three tallest towers, reading from left to right, are the white spire of City Hall, the Gothic steeple of Bermuda Cathedral, and the extraordinary campanile-style superstructure of Sessions House, home of the Assembly and the Supreme Court.

The forested island in the inner harbor midway between Hamilton and Paget, WHITE'S

Loll on the grass, take in the sun at Bermuda's Botanical Gardens.

ISLAND, was leased to the United States as a navy base during World War I. Later it failed as a tourist resort. The Bermuda Sailboat Club rescued it from decay after World War II, and it's now a center of local youth activities, with the emphasis on boating.

The commuter ferry from Hamilton makes five stops along this shore, the middle one at SALT KETTLE. A small hotel on the harbor's edge, the Glencoe, was the vacation home of Woodrow Wilson in 1912, between his election as U.S. president and his inauguration.

Another traditional harbor-front hotel further along the shore, the **Inverurie**, is much bigger than it looks. Two modern sections of the hotel are hidden across the road. Among the amenities is a harborside terrace on which bands and nightclub acts perform under the stars—sometimes attracting an appreciative but non-paying audience aboard small boats and yachts which anchor just offshore to share the fun.

The **Belmont Hotel,** in Warwick parish, stands as a pink landmark overlooking the harbor from a hilltop in the middle of its own 110-acre estate. This is one of Bermuda's big,

46

By Moped Round Bermuda

Puttering about Bermuda by moped can be exhilarating, but don't dash off on your rented vehicle until you've read this:

● Be sure the rental agency explains the machine and you fully understand how to start, drive and stop it. Test drive it under supervision until you feel confident.

● You must wear the crash helmet provided.

● Dress for comfort and protection: no bathing suits, no bare feet. Wear proper shoes. Take along a windbreaker. Sunglasses are good protection in case of flying insects or gravel.

● Keep reminding yourself to drive on the left, especially at roundabouts and after a break in the trip.

● Eyes front: don't worry about the traffic behind you. The locals approach tourists with caution.

● When you're not aboard the bike, lock it.

self-contained resort hotels with its own 18-hole golf course, not to mention all the other sports facilities, restaurants, nightclubs and so on. For ocean swimming the guests are taken to a private beach half a mile away on the south shore.

The view from the Belmont encompasses the principal harbor islands. The nearest, HINSON ISLAND, is inhabited by the owners of some enviable homes, who choose to escape what they consider the hectic pace of the "mainland". They can commute for business or shopping on the ferryboat.

In the harbor due west of the Belmont, DARRELL ISLAND has lived through eras of glory and despair. It was used as a quarantine station for arriving ships, then as a tent camp for 1,000 prisoners during the Boer War. Just before the outbreak of World War II it became a vital refuelling station for transatlantic clippers, with a million-dollar seaplane terminal. But long-distance land-based planes were developed, and a runway was laid out at the east end of the colony, sinking the flying boat business. After the war Darrell Island bounced back. The old hangars were turned into sound stages for television films. Somehow Hollywood survived the competition and Bermuda's show-biz island failed. Perhaps the next idea-man will have better luck.

Harbour Road turns inland to stay clear of a peninsula pointing westward from Warwick. This is the home of the **Riddell's Bay Golf and Country Club,** something of a historic monument, having been founded in 1922. At 5,476 yards, Bermuda's oldest course is slightly shorter than the Belmont's but no less scenic.

Now Harbour Road runs into Middle Road, which continues westward. Just offshore you'll notice PEROT'S ISLAND, a luxuriously developed private island, and SPECTACLE ISLAND, resembling a pair of eyeglasses in shape.

At BLACK BAY the offshore scenery is somewhat forlorn: the remains of two old ships, a coal lighter and a freighter. They didn't run ashore here, but were towed to this point and then abandoned.

South Coast Sights

Less than a mile to the west, South Road merges with Middle Road; Bermuda's Main Island is now so narrow it has room for only one thoroughfare instead of the three parallel routes we began with. This might be the logical moment to double back on South Road, heading eastward again, to see some of the sights along the sunny south coast. This is a long stretch of rocky headlands interrupted by beaches big and small, including the legendary pink beaches of the tourist brochures. The casuarinas bend and whistle in the wind and giant sea grape shrubs flourish in sandy adversity.

CHURCH BAY is not one of the famous beaches but it's a pleasing enough strand more than 100 yards long, backed by a grassy hill. There are ruins of an old fort, dated 1612, and not-so-historic picnic facilities in good repair.

The **Sonesta Beach Hotel** stands astride a peninsula separating two small sandy bays —BOAT BAY and SINKY BAY. Taking advantage of its position as the only major hotel with a couple of beaches right on the premises, the Sonesta accents water sports and ocean views. It has its own undersea observatory and an unusual year-round swimming pool under a glass dome.

From here the great white landmark visible from as far away as Hamilton, the **Gibb's Hill Lighthouse,** looms almost overhead, at the top of Lighthouse Road. Enthusiasts of spiral staircases won't want

Gibbs Hill Lighthouse surveys the beauties of Bermuda: 150 islands

and islets set in a deep blue sea.

to miss the 185 steps up the inside of the tower. The reward is a 360-degree panorama from the obstruction-free gangway around the outside near the top of the structure. Take a map with you and compare it with the reality of these far-flung islands and islets. Of course the lighthouse has a much more serious function. It warns ships as much as 40 miles away that they're approaching Bermuda's dangerous reefs. The cast iron build-

Revel in sun, sea and sand at Elbow Beach (left) or Horseshoe Bay.

ing was prefabricated in England in 1844 and shipped safely through the Bermuda reefs to be assembled atop Gibb's Hill (alt. 245 feet). The light is thus 362 feet above sea level. Several sources of fuel have been used, most recently electricity; when this fails, emergency generators light the

1,500-watt bulb. And if they, too, fail, radio warnings are sent to all ships at sea that Bermuda has gone invisible. Lighthouse keepers no longer have to wind the machinery that turns the magnifying lens or trim the wicks of the light. It's all automated except for polishing the brass.

With room for more than 1,000 guests, the **Southampton Princess Hotel,** on a hill overlooking the south coast, is Bermuda's biggest resort complex. The $50-million establishment, opened in 1972, has its own 18-hole par-three golf course and nearby beach and beach club, indoor and outdoor pools, day and night tennis courts, and under one roof, a variety of shops, restaurants, bars and nightclubs.

Horseshoe Bay, a public beach east of the 60-acre spread of the Southampton Princess, is a solid contender for any list of the world's ten most perfect beaches. This sublime arc of powdery white sand extends a quarter of a mile, edging a blue-green sea. Rock formations at the extremities of the sweep of beach, and jutting out of the middle of the bay, add visual excitement—and interesting possibilities for snorkelers and fishermen.

From Horseshoe Bay eastward stretch several more splendid beaches, separated by rocky outcrops. Here the turquoise inshore sea seems even more remarkable because it ends suddenly at a certain depth, where conventional blue-gray waters begin. Just offshore all along the south

coast are Bermuda's fascinating but perilous "boilers". The word dating from Elizabethan times describes the circular reefs over which the troubled surf boils.

Many military bases tend to be built on land nobody wants, in desolate corners even nature seems to have abandoned. Not so with WARWICK CAMP, the headquarters of Bermu-

The islands boast beaches galore, some secluded, others easy of access, none more impressive than the majestic sweep of Warwick Long Bay.

da's self-defense forces, which overlooks the beautiful south coast. The Bermuda Regiment, mostly part-time conscripts, holds exercises—even target practice—at times. But the public is always warned and sentries keep anyone from straying into danger.

Warwick Long Bay lies safely beyond rifle range. This half-mile-long beach adjoins a park with hiking trails and bridle paths. One of Bermuda's romantic sights is the vision of a troop of horses being exercised along the shore, wading into the sea for a refreshing splash.

Most of the lovely pink beaches found intermittently to the east of Warwick Long Bay are private, either belonging to hotels or operated as clubs. Several, though, admit the public for a fee. The **Elbow Beach Hotel,** for instance, allows outsiders to use the facilities of its surf club and famous quarter-mile pastel beach. Elbow Beach, whose well-recognized symbol is a top-hatted sea-horse; started before World War I as a small guest house; now its main building, cottages and lanais accommodate hundreds of guests. The hotel issues a catalogue of 150 types of plants found on its 29 acres.

The next hotel up the line is much newer, and novel in its premise. The **Stonington Beach Hotel,** a small resort with attractive landscaping and architecture, is owned and operated by the Bermuda College. The clerks, cooks, waiters and housemaids are local students learning the hotel business; every day is an exam. Since they're under close supervision and great pressure to succeed, the service tends to be more enthusiastic than in "ordinary" hotels. And, after all, even old professional waiters and bartenders sometimes drop a glass.

To the Tip of the Hook

People who have stared long enough at a map of Bermuda usually conclude that it resembles a fishhook or a beckoning finger. The tip of the hook, or finger, is the northern end of Ireland Island. To get there we pick up the westward itinerary again in Southampton parish, where South Road merges with Middle Road. From that intersection it's less than 10 miles to the end of the line.

At FRANK'S BAY cyclists may take a detour (a shortcut, actually) running off to the right. This tranquil path is one of several offbeat lanes covering what used to be the right-of-way of the Bermuda Railway. The ambitious project, inaugurated in 1931, provided public transportation over almost the entire length of the colony; the tracks went right down Front Street in Hamilton. In retrospect most Bermudians agree it was a great idea, but in 1947, when the automobile seemed to be a panacea, the railway was scrapped. Now it would cost many times the original price to revive the picturesque, eminently sensible Bermuda Railway.

After the cycle path rejoins

the main road, it's less than half a mile to Whale Bay Road, a minor artery going off to the left. This leads to WEST WHALE BAY, a rather isolated park with a small sand beach and a ruined fort. In the days of Bermuda's whaling industry this was one of the important centers of the trade. The boatsmen, harpooners and oil dealers enjoyed prosperity for nearly a century; the last whaling company went out of business in the 1880s.

The government-run **Port Royal Golf Course** is open to the public. Designed by the Robert Trent Jones organization, the 6,541-yard layout takes advantage of the spectacular coastal scenery. It's been in operation since 1970.

Roughly opposite the entrance to the golf course you can find another of those flowered cycle paths bequeathed by the railway. Part of this one runs through the property of the U.S. Naval Air Station Annex, which extends into Great Sound on an artificial peninsula created from two islands and a mighty heap of landfill.

Near the entrance to the base is the frontier between Southampton and Sandys parishes. Sandys (usually pronounced in the British way, with the "y" silent) includes a last chunk of Main Island and all the rest of the archipelago to the tip of the hook. Main Island, which we are about to leave for the first time in this itinerary, is about 14 miles long and vastly bigger than any of the other islands now linked with it by bridges.)

A road going off to the left, before Somerset Bridge, bears the intriguing name of Wreck Road. It comes to an end at the edge of a private estate

Cheep Thrills
Among the hardy migratory birds that schedule refuelling stops in Bermuda is the Tropic Bird, aptly nicknamed the Longtail for its graceful white trailing tail.

A noisy native is the Cahow bird, protected on the islands of Castle Harbour after nearly becoming extinct. Another fixture, widely seen and loudly heard all around Bermuda is the yellow-breasted Kiskadee (the name imitates its assertive call). Cardinals and bluebirds round out the brilliant color scheme.

When the birds quiet down at night the loud little frogs let go. Bermuda's inch-long tree frogs, imported from the West Indies a century ago, chirp like bells. But when you come close enough to investigate, they clam up.

occupying an entire peninsula with stupendous views of the ocean and Ely's Harbour. **Wreck Hill** is where local folk, once upon a time, are alleged to have lit fires on stormy nights to lure foreign ships to their doom on the reefs. Of course the islanders were experts at salvage operations or, if it came to that, piracy. Even in more ethical modern times Wreck Hill has been a lookout point—for spotting potential customers for local tugboats.

Somerset Bridge, then, must be crossed to leave Main Island. If you weren't paying attention you might bounce across this bridge without realizing it's one of Bermuda's most fetching and photographed attractions. It lays claim to a world record of engaging modesty: the world's smallest drawbridge. The part that flips up (by hand) is less than two feet across—just wide enough to permit a sailboat's mast to go through. It's such fun you may want to hang around for a maritime traffic jam. (Another way to reach Somerset Bridge is by sea: The ferryboat from Hamilton stops there.)

Somerset Island's diminutive drawbridge is as pretty as a picture.

Somerset Island

Astride the narrowest part of Somerset Island, **Fort Scaur** is a 19th-century redoubt that feels as solid as Gibraltar. From the top of the battlements—where an antiaircraft gun was mounted, just in case, during World War II—you can see both ends of the island. The archipelago from here looks like a snake about to attack its own tail. Fort Scaur was built to defend the Dockyard on Ireland Island from any attack by the Americans in the War of 1812. By now all the war scars and even the old guns are gone. What remains is 22 acres of prime parkland, with picnic tables on the parade ground lawn. But you can explore the tunnels which prove what a beehive the fort once was. All the guidebooks recommend looking for the so-called Lonely Milestone, inscribed "London 3076 Miles", with "27th Regiment, R.E. 1906" on the reverse. The Bermuda historian Terry Tucker punctures the usual romantic explanation that it's the work of a homesick British soldier. Instead she asserts that the Royal Engineers erected such milestones in other parts of Bermuda, as well, to practice calculating distances. It was official business.

Mrs. Tucker has also written extensively about a bizarre century-old murder case centered on SKEETERS CORNER, near the western tip of Somerset Island. Edward Skeeters was a local man whose vanished wife was the object of a wide search. The case would have remainded forever a mystery if bored off-duty fishermen scanning the horizon hadn't noticed a curious tidal effect not far offshore. There they found the body. Skeeters confessed to the murder and was hanged. With grave poetic justice he was buried beneath the great stone he had used to sink the body of his victim.

DANIEL'S HEAD, the peninsula beyond Skeeters Corner, is occupied by yet another military base, this one the Canadian Forces Station Bermuda. It's a naval communications base, established in 1963.

Somerset Long Bay is the biggest and best public beach of the west end—a couple of hundred yards of blinding white sand that looks and feels like finely ground seashells. Although it faces the open sea, the beach has a gradual shallow slope suitable for small children's fun and games. Backing the bay is a reserve of the Audubon Society.

Tranquility is a Somerset specialty.

The next peninsula is the domain of **Cambridge Beaches,** an exclusive cottage colony with several private beaches. Founded in the 1920s, this was the first hostelry in the distinctive Bermuda style with the living quarters spread over the landscape.

The village of **Somerset,** with a handful of shops along a narrow main road, caters to tourists who are escaping from the "big city" atmosphere of Hamilton. The shopping here is certainly relaxed, and unusually sophisticated for a whistle-stop village. Mangrove Bay, once a port for smugglers, attracts many pleasure boats these days. Palm trees shade the long narrow beach but all the mangrove trees are gone.

Near Watford Bridge, at the eastern end of the village, an odd little obelisk commemorates soldiers who died not in battle but during a pneumonia epidemic in 1916. There's a ferry station on the Somerset side of Watford Bridge.

Before leaving Somerset Island, though, two historic buildings deserve a look. **St. James's Church** is an 18th-century parish church, much rebuilt because of hurricanes and other problems. Its graceful spire and whitewashed walls make the church a striking sight.

Surrounded by the **Gilbert Nature Reserve,** the old manse named **Springfield** is a proud example of an 18th-century

Bermuda planter's residence. It's now used as the Somerset branch of the Bermuda Library.

Tiny WATFORD ISLAND, across the bridge from Somerset Island, and the next link in the archipelago, BOAZ ISLAND, hold memories of the unfortunate convicts sent out from Britain in the 19th century to build the Dockyard project. Most lived aboard prison hulks anchored at the other end of the colony, but the overflow was assigned to barracks on Boaz Island. The ones who died, mostly in epidemics, were buried on Watford Island.

59

Ireland Island

Finally to Ireland Island, the end of the line. Once the Gibraltar of the West, its mountain of military strength has shrunk to a melancholy molehill. Only a handful of British naval personnel are left, manning a station called H.M.S. Malabar, the Royal Navy's last remaining foothold on this side of the Atlantic. But echoes of imperial power linger on Ireland Island, from the Royal Navy cemetery in a delightful glade to the Commissioner's House, a 150-year-old pomposity which cost more than £50,000.

Ireland Island's potential as a naval outpost came to the fore at the beginning of the 19th century. Not only was Britain fighting Napoleon, but there were fears that the government of the new United States coveted Bermuda. Ireland Island was almost uninhabited when the Admiralty bought it, and so isolated from the "civilized" east end of the colony that there was no resistance to the project. But in 1810 construction of a major mid-ocean dockyard began.

That old symbol of Britannia has been put to new use as the center of a rejuvenated community. In a setting animated by the beat retreats of the Bermuda Regiment Band and the clip-clopping of horse-drawn carriages, the **Royal Naval Dockyard's** historic buildings, museums, shopping center and craft market are attracting more and more tourists.

On the way into the dockyard area you'll pass the unmarked entrance to Casemates Prison on your left. This formidable fortress-penitentiary served many military purposes before it became Bermuda's maximum security prison in recent years.

With twin 100-foot stone towers, the vast **East Storehouse** of the dockyard resembles some misplaced Spanish convent. If time and tide wait for no man, this would be the place to check on the state of the race. One tower houses a four-way clock, the other was designed to indicate the tide schedule.

The Keepyard of this old naval base, occupying the northern extremity of Ireland Island, has been rescued from abandonment and developed into Bermuda's biggest and best museum. Queen Elizabeth II officially opened the **Bermuda Maritime Museum** in 1975 but it has greatly expanded since then.

There's much to see in the

main building, the **Queen's Exhibition Hall,** originally designed to hold thousands of barrels of gunpowder. Under its vaulted brick ceiling are ship models large and small, old maps, and a whaling exhibit accompanied by a recording of humpback whales "singing"—a cross between a foghorn and the wail of a lonely child.

An even older building, the so-called **Treasure House,** is concerned with marine archaeology, including the history of deep-sea diving. Many relics salvaged from old wrecks are on show, especially the fabulous haul of gold and jewels discovered in 1955 by the local diver Teddy Tucker. The best of his find, thought to come from a Spanish galleon sunk in 1593, is displayed behind burglar-proof glass. These precautions were undertaken a little late, though. Just before the Queen was due to inspect the museum it was discovered that a priceless bishop's cross mounted with seven emeralds had been purloined; a plastic replica had been left behind. The real one is still missing.

In other buildings of the museum you can see exhibits on the Royal Navy's presence in Bermuda, old sailboats

Divers comb the Bermuda reefs for treasure. Many a historic old wreck waits to be discovered.

undergoing restoration and a gleamingly polished Bermuda fitted dinghy nearly a century old. (These traditional craft, of which several are still in **61** use, are noted for their immense sail area, the large size of their crew, and problems of balance.) An exhibit on Bermuda pilots includes a real gig—a sleek boat rowed by six or eight men to rush the pilots out to arriving ships far offshore. Astonishingly, these man-propelled speedboats were in use here until 1929.

Out on the parade ground, the big statue of Neptune was the figurehead of the old battleship, *H. M. S. Irresistible*, scrapped in Bermuda in 1891. In the mid-20th century King Neptune, resolutely holding his trident, was hauled to the Dockyard by helicopter and put on display.

You can wander the ramparts surrounding the keep, and have a look at the Commissioner's House with its cast-iron balconies. The ongoing restoration program has managed to return the early 19th-century mansion to its original overblown grandeur.

From the ramparts, gaze out upon Bermuda's **Sea Gardens,** where the coral reefs are protected by law. Glass-bottom boat tours from various Bermuda ports come out to the coral wonderworld—part of it just a clam's throw from the Ireland Island fortifications.

Eastward from Hamilton

The parish of Devonshire, east of the capital, has fewer hotel rooms than any other parish but a little bit of almost every type of Bermuda scenery— steep hills, marshy lowland, beaches and cliffs, and some delightful back roads lined with hibiscus, bougainvillea and morning glory.

Less than a mile out of town on Middle Road is a way-station for nature-lovers, the **Arboretum.** This 20-acre park with lovely old trees is cool and appealing. Note the old stone quarry now turned into a sunken tropical garden.

Bermudians are fond of one of their oldest churches, across Middle Road from Devonshire Marsh. You could easily miss it, for a bigger, much newer church—*only* 130 years old— stares you in the face. The "new" church is quite appealing in its own right, with a high-pitched roof. Inside, the ceiling looks like an upturned ship's hull. And it was ship's carpenters who built **Old Devonshire Church,** the small cottage-style building in the churchyard a couple of hundred yards away. The first church on the site, roofed with thatched palmetto leaves, was built in 1623. The present building dates from 1716, and was generally known as Brackish Pond Church, for its location next to the marsh.

Between the marsh and the north coast, the **Ocean View Golf and Country Club** (formerly Queen's Park) manages to squeeze in nine short but challenging holes of golf. This is Bermuda's other government-owned course, open to the public.

South Coast

On the south coast, **Devonshire Bay** is a slim strand of sand at the end of a small bay almost completely enclosed by protective rocks. Here you can watch the little fishing boats come in to unload the catch; notice the sign warning that "the cleaning of fish is permitted only near boat ramp" and going on to ban "drunkardness"—perhaps a fisherman's failing. On South Road near the turnoff to Devonshire Bay you'll pass **Palm Grove Garden,** a singularly sumptuous private park.

Smith's parish, east of Devonshire, is the least populous parish in the colony but the highest. It boasts Bermuda's tallest eminence, TOWN HILL, 259 feet above sea level and sometimes known as the Peak.

On a lesser hilltop stands **Verdmont,** a worthy old Bermuda house now furnished with most interesting antiques. The house, a property of the Bermuda National Trust, is either 200 or 300 years old, depending on which version you hear. But there's no quibbling over the architectural ingenuity. Its eight fireplaces are all different, and so are the giant andirons; the chimneys project beyond the walls. The large sash windows have inside shutters—most unusual in Bermuda. The noble central staircase goes all the way up to the oversized attic with its unique double-tiered roof. Among the alluring antiques on show are a four-poster bed, two early pianos, a surprisingly good collection of ceramics from China, and in the nursery, delightful old toys, including an ancient child's scooter with cast-iron wheels. The slave quarters, kitchens and toilets were all assigned separate outbuildings. Incidentally, the present visitors' entrance to Verdmont is through the "back" door, on the north side.

Back on South Road, notice two unusual churches. St. Patrick's Roman Catholic Church is Bermuda's only circular church, strikingly modern, with a huge bas-relief sculp- **63**

ture of the patron saint over the main door. Farther east, **St. Mark's Church,** the Smith's parish church, looks quite ancient though it's less than 150 years old. The setting is inspiringly bucolic.

The **Spittal Pond Nature Reserve,** a joint project of the National Trust and the Audubon Society, ought to quicken the pulses of bird-watchers. Any time of year the fragrant shady walks are alive with warblers, but in spring and fall migratory birds join the society. Spittal Pond itself, a favorite landing strip for waterfowl, is fenced off but close enough for surveillance.

Along the shoreline are some weird rock formations and cactus backed by pine trees. The man-made memento people come to look at is an inscription on what's called **Spanish Rock.** A legendary Spanish (maybe Portuguese) sailor made his mark here–in 1543. Inspired by this bid for immortality, legions of modern graffiti artists have dug in to emulate and outdo him. The historical inscription can be read in bronze on the spot—or in a clear copy in the Bermuda Historical Society Museum in Hamilton.

Heading east from the bird sanctuary, South Road hugs the dramatic coastline, soon disclosing **John Smith's Bay.** This much-photographed, perfect patch of pink sand is named after the English Captain John Smith, the 17th-century adventurer. Though he

Eyebrows and Moongates

To appreciate the architectural inventiveness of the Bermudians, it helps to know the lingo:

Buttery. A small square outbuilding with steep pyramidal whitewashed roof; perishable food was kept cool within its thick walls.

Eyebrows. Arched protrusions over windows or doors, to relieve the square design and perhaps deflect rain.

Moongate. Circular stone gates said to bring good luck to passers-through, the design imported from China by an old Bermuda sea captain.

Story-and-a-half. A house built into a hillside, with the main floor on top and a half-floor beneath.

Welcoming arms. Outside stairway to upper (main) floor, built (as if for perspective) narrower at the door. Slaves lived on the lower floor with separate entrance.

St. Mark's Church, a venerable stronghold of the Anglican faith.

never set foot on Bermuda, the colony's connection with Virginia has always been close. Smith is remembered for having been saved from death by the Indian Princess Pocahontas. Later she married John Rolfe, one of the Virginia settlers who survived the Bermuda shipwreck of the *Sea Venture.* Small world.

Around Harrington Sound

Less than a quarter of a mile north of John Smith's Bay is Harrington Sound, an inland sea very popular with boatmen of all stripes. When conditions are too rough beyond Bermuda's shores, it's usually clear sailing in the sound; and many of the fish who come in to visit decide to stay. The southernmost end of the sound is the site of **Devil's Hole,** Bermuda's first tourist attraction. For more than 150 years the owners of this collapsed cave have been showing off the curiosity—and charging admission since 1843. What makes Devil's Hole different from the other caves which ring Harrington Sound is the contents

Ponder the wonders of the deep: at the Aquarium (left), or looking out on Harrington Sound.

of the deep natural pool: a school of fish who've been hopelessly spoiled. Visitors toss out baited but hookless lines for the excitement of catching big and little fish and turtles; of course the fearless fauna merely eat the bait and go in peace, but not without a bit of a tussle.

Harrington Sound's only obvious link with the ocean is Flatts Inlet, where the changes of tide are always magnified by the waters rushing beneath the narrow bridge. Once a haunt of smugglers avoiding officials at Hamilton or St. George's, this pleasant little harbor now hosts dozens of law-abiding small boats. **Flatts Village** is still a center of maritime activities, with the emphasis on water sports, including a unique attraction—diving helmets for underwater walks. A fixture of the low-lying, lazy scenery here is a famous small hotel, the Coral Island, which goes down to the water's edge.

The small uninhabited island at the entrance to Flatts Inlet is named GIBBET ISLAND or Gallows Island, and for good reason. The isle used to be the site of public hangings.

On the north side of the inlet, Bermuda's **Aquarium** is

open 364 days a year (the fish take Christmas off). The show features creatures as lovable as parrotfish and angelfish, and villains like the vast blue-eyed green moray eel. At no extra charge you can take a radio-controlled "guided tour" of the tank area, hanging onto an "audio wand" conveying a commentary by experts. A beautiful display of living coral and big fish in a 40,000-gallon tank is excited now and again by artificial waves, created to convince the coral they're still at sea.

Outside, the Aquarium runs a creditable sideline—a zoo and aviary. If you have time, watch the spontaneous turtle races, involving a family of a

Life in Flatt's Village, once a hideout for smugglers, revolves around a spick-and-span fleet of fishing boats and a pleasant resort hotel.

dozen or so lumbering Galapagos tortoises; these huge landlubber reptiles thrive in the Bermuda environment. Their companions in the zoo include some engaging monkeys in airy cages and a languid passel of alligators. There's a fine exhibition of multicolored tropical birds. The cockatoos and giant macaws say "hello" and "sorry" to each other.

From here North Shore Road continues on a narrow strip of land separating Harrington Sound Road from the Atlantic. This is Hamilton parish, with the islands' lowest population density but a goodly share of the tourist attractions. Off to the left you'll be delighted at the sight of **Shelly Bay**, with its quiet wa-

Brilliant multi-colored tropical birds steal the show at the Bermuda Zoo's aviary.

ters evolving from gray to green to emerald. The beach, nearly 200 yards long, is open to the public, as is a recreation ground beyond.

The road climbs steadily along Crawl Hill, named after the corrals or *kraals* which used to be set in the sea near here to trap fish. Horse-drawn vehicles and bikes ascend the steep slope at a slow pace.

Coming down the hill the road curves around the end of BAILEY'S BAY; notice the piers jutting from the water, the remains of a bridge by which the old Bermuda Railway used to take a shortcut across the bay. At the intersection of North Shore Road and the charmingly named Fractious Street, the **Bermuda Museum** concentrates on the life and times of notable Bermudians. The house is filled with old Bermuda furniture, accessories and handicrafts.

The next of the Bailey's Bay area sights is a small **perfume factory** set in a cheerful garden. If the real-life zephyrs of Bermuda weren't already so fragrant, entering the sweet atmosphere of this cottage industry would be even more impressive. Guided tours offer a glimpse of the production process—which can take up to 18 months. Among the scents bottled here: passion flower, Easter lily, oleander, jasmine and sweet pea.

The stretch of land between Harrington Sound and Castle Harbour is riddled with caves, one of them on the grounds of the **Grotto Bay Beach and Tennis Club.** This posh gardened hotel complex is just across the causeway from the airport. As for the grotto, it's been rigged up as a disco, called Prospero's Cave.

Crystal Caves, discovered in 1907, make the most of the drama of stalagmites and dripping stalactites. Hidden lights point out the shapes of natural sculptures among the ancient pillars. A pontoon bridge crosses a pool of eerily clear, still water reflecting the limestone formations hanging from the ceiling. The spectacular nether-world radiates an unearthly greenish glow. Nature works its wonders in unhurried fashion—the formations take on a mere cubic inch in a hundred years.

The competition, down the road, is **Leamington Caves.** Here, too, lighting effects dramatize the fantasy underworld.

The amber-tinted grotto features nearly two acres of crystal formations and a number of underground pools connecting to a lake.

You don't have to be a keen spelunker to explore these two Bermuda caves; there are clearly defined paths and hand rails, and guides to answer questions.

More caves are part of the Walsingham property on Walsingham Bay near Leamington Caves. The fine old house known as **Walsingham** was built more than 300 years ago. Among the lush vegetation on the property is a calabash tree alluded to by Thomas Moore in one of his Bermuda poems. Though he never lived in the house, it's now called Tom Moore's Tavern and operates as a restaurant.

Perfect timing as a trainer puts dolphins through their paces. Bermuda's marine life is one of the island's great drawing cards.

Castle Harbour Area

The **Castle Harbour,** the vast hotel which rounds out the territory of Hamilton parish, is said to be the largest privately-owned property in Bermuda. Its 260 acres encompass a traditional hotel with modern annexes, 18-hole golf course, tennis courts, pools, two beaches and a yacht club. Developed by the Furness-Withy Steamship Line, the Castle Harbour opened in opulence in 1931. During the war it housed some of the men building the American air base across the harbor. Since then, the hotel has been expanded; today it is among Bermuda's largest.

waste your time looking for the town hall, main square or any other municipal premises. The town was a dream of 17th-century Governor Daniel Tucker, all on paper. In the 1920s property developers bought up the land and Tucker's Town became the colony's most exclusive residential area. The center of social life for the neighborhood is the **Mid-Ocean Club** with its championship 18-hole golf course. The club has air-conditioned apartments for guests, but only members and their friends are eligible to stay there. The club is sufficiently discreet and isolated to have been chosen as the site for Anglo-American summit conferences.

One of Bermuda's natural curiosities, alongside the club's private pink beach, is signposted. **Natural Arches** (left), a phenomenon unlikely to produce squeals of wonderment, remains a popular place to take pictures. The stone archways are said to be the last vestiges of a cave, the rest of which collapsed into the sea long before Bermuda was inhabited.

Just off the tip of the peninsula is CASTLE ISLAND, once a key installation in the defense of Castle Harbour. In 1614, when two Spanish ships came

In what might appear to be old-fashioned gerrymandering, the peninsula running to the east beyond the hotel has been bureaucratically detached from Hamilton parish and linked to St. George's parish a couple of miles across Castle Harbour. The road signs all point to TUCKER'S TOWN, but don't

in to find out what the British were up to, it was the Castle Island battery which sent them packing with two shots.

A much larger island, also at the harbor entrance, NONSUCH ISLAND, is a bird sanctuary which preserves species of flora and fauna which have been threatened elsewhere. Fifty years ago Nonsuch was the headquarters of the pioneer undersea explorer, Dr. William Beebe, and his bathysphere.

U.S. Naval Air Station

To reach the remainder of St. George's parish—including Bermuda's most historic area —you have to go all the way around the harbor to the causeway. This is the only bridge between the east end and Main Island. The original span was opened in 1871 but wrecked by a hurricane and tidal wave at the turn of the century. The concrete replacement is still in use, but the swing bridge at the eastern end is a fairly recent addition. On windy days the mile-long causeway is ticklish going for cyclists, and the final bridge must be approached with caution; note the cycle lane marked down the middle of the grating.

During World War II the topography and character of the east end of the colony underwent a drastic change. An American air base was built on a composite of a dozen islands and islets, with the gaps filled in by nearly a square mile of land reclaimed from the sea. Since 1946 commercial airliners have shared the runway with the military planes. The U.S. Naval Air Station, a community of several thousand military, dependents and civilian employees, is best known for its anti-submarine patrols and search-and-rescue missions undertaken when shipwrecks occur.

The Civil Air Terminal is just past the end of the causeway. To reach the main gate of the Naval Air Station, you have to go all the way around to the north side of the runways. Visitors are allowed onto the base to inspect **Carter Historic House,** an old Bermuda building which has survived all the wartime and postwar upheaval. This old stone cottage with hand-hewn cedar beams and a sagging roof is thought to date from the mid-17th century. The Carter who built it was a descendant of Christopher Carter, one of the original two settlers who stayed behind on Bermuda after the

Sea Venture survivors settled in Jamestown. You must stop at the main gate for a pass before proceeding to Carter House, either by free base bus or by motorbike. Note that the Navy forbids cyclists to drive on the station unless they wear glasses or eyeshields, as a safety requirement.

At the southeastern extremity of the airbase, on what used to be a separate island called Cooper's Island, is the Bermuda **tracking station** of N.A.S.A., the U.S. space agency. The outpost, employing several dozen American technicians and an equal number of locally hired personnel, has participated in all the U.S. manned space flights, as well as unmanned scientific and military missions. The technicians have also been involved in many other projects, including a study of wildfowl migration; radar can be fine-tuned to distinguish a goose from a grouse. If you'd like a close look at all those antennas, shaped like saucers, corkscrews, poles and wire baskets—as well as a nice little fringe benefit called N.A.S.A. beach—you can arrange to visit the establishment. Entry is through the main gate of the Navy base, where you must obtain a pass.

St. David's Island

A public road goes along the northern boundary of the airport just outside the high wire fence paralleling the main runway. The thin civilian foothold between the fence and the waterfront sometimes widens enough to leave room for hamlets of modest cottages. The people who live from here to the end of the peninsula gave up half their island to the war effort... a terrible wrench for any islanders. In part because of their long isolation, St. David's Island folk have always been different from other Bermudians. Until 1934 when the Severn Bridge was opened, they had to take a ferry to get to the rest of the world (St. George's)—and many never bothered to go as far as Hamilton, much less America. Some islanders have a distinctive facial structure and complexion which is believed to identify them as descendants of North American Indians brought to Bermuda as slaves. St. David's islanders, whatever their roots, have always been rugged, uninhibited seafaring folk—fishermen, sailors, whalers, pilots, blockaderunners and pirates. Gourmets from all over Bermuda rave about the seafood here.

At the easternmost point of

Bermuda, **Great Head Park** mixes forest, walking trails and extensive fortifications. Rusted cannon hang with drooping barrels, abandoned but for shy lizards; you might take the ensemble for an anti-war sculpture.

Overlooking all of this is **St. David's Lighthouse,** newer and shorter than Bermuda's No. 1 lighthouse on Main Island. If you have to go into the lighthouse-keeping business, this is a congenial place for it—a tidy pink cottage alongside the tower, surrounded by a six-acre park, with dozens of neighbors nearby and a super view of the ocean, the airport and the space-age skyline of the N.A.S.A. tracking station.

The Severn Bridge, which first established permanent all-weather contact between St. David's and the rest of the colony, lasted only 17 years. It was condemned as a safety hazard; you can still see the unlovely piers wading across the strait. To reach St. George's Island now you have to go back to the main gate of the navy base, around the traffic circle (clockwise!) and over the Swing Bridge.

If you were to turn left at the end of Mullet Bay, Ferry Road would lead you past the Bermuda Biological Station. Founded in 1932, this research and educational organization keeps an eye on and under Bermuda's coral sea. But the main road swings right and follows Mullet Bay, with its flock of small boats at anchor. From here it's only a mile to the center of St. George's, a town of carefully preserved historic ambience, just made for strolling.

Davy Jones & Co.

Lighthouses or not, Bermuda has always been an infamous graveyard for ships. Over the centuries the tricky barrier reefs almost encircling the colony have undone more than 300 ships. And in spite of all the modern navigational aids, it still happens from time to time, in a storm or accident.

From Spanish galleons to paddle-wheeled blockade-runners, the wrecks fascinate modern treasure-hunters in scuba gear.

Bermuda's coat-of-arms shows a shipwreck—the demise of the *Sea Venture.* The 17th-century artist imagined the ship colliding with a cliff much bigger than any available in Bermuda, but the symbolism remains pertinent for many an anxious sailor approaching the former "Isles of Devils".

St. George's Town

Bermuda's original capital, founded in 1612, is so small you can't get lost, but it's a good idea to call at the Visitors Service Bureau facing King's Square for a free map and leaflet with directions for a "self-guided walking experience". It hits the high-spots of St. George's in an easy itinerary which starts across the bridge on **Ordnance Island.**

There, dwarfed by visiting cruise ships, trawlers or freighters, an old wooden sailing ship has been recreated—a replica of **Deliverance,** one of the rescue ships built by survivors of the original wreck of the *Sea Venture.* The sturdy little makeshift ship made the risky crossing to Jamestown, Virginia, in May, 1610. If you go aboard the replica you'll share the claustrophobia the colonists must have experienced, crammed into *Deliverance;* steerage was luxury compared to this! The Ordnance Island **ducking stool,** also a replica, is used on occasion to simulate the punishment meted out to chronic gossips 300 years ago—but just for the amusement of the tourists.

Back on the "mainland", **King's Square** provides another of those irresistible pic-

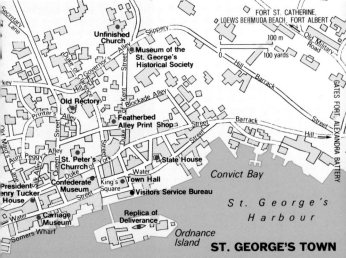

ture possibilities—the chance to have your photo taken "imprisoned" in the stocks.

Twin exterior stairways contribute to the harmonious design of the **Town Hall,** a restored 18th-century building on the square. On Saturdays from December to March the Lord Mayor, with the chain of office hanging round his neck, shakes hands with all the tourists while the town crier rings his bell and formalizes the Bermuda Rendezvous festivities. Whether your greeting is ceremonious or casual, notice the Bermuda cedar furnishings inside the hall.

Old State House, near the Town Hall—the colony's first all-stone structure—was built in 1620. Originally known as Sessions House, it was the first permanent home of the colonial assembly, which until then had held its debates in St. Peter's Church. When the capital was shifted to Hamilton the historic building was turned over to the Masonic lodge, which still pays a symbolic rent of one peppercorn a year. The ritual of the peppercorn payment, in April, is one of the islands' colorful occasions.

The heart of Sir George Somers, commander of the *Sea Venture* expedition of 1609, is buried in **Somers Gardens,** a small tropical park.

Up the hill you may glimpse what looks like some medieval monastic relic, perhaps the victim of earthquake or fire. But it's only St. George's "Unfinished Church", a century-old folly. When the islands' first church, St. Peter's, began to show grave signs of wear, eager parishioners promoted the construction of a new stone edifice with somber gothic lines. But before the project could reach fulfillment everyone agreed that the orig-

Town Hall, St. George's: sightseeing by moped makes sense.

inal church, with its fundamental historical connections, shouldn't be sacrificed. Still roofless, the "new" church was abandoned and St. Peter's was restored instead. Palm trees flourish in and around the ruins and the lawns are kept tidy, but don't come too close in case some more masonry falls off.

The **St. George's Historical Society Museum,** in an early 18th-century house, provides a comprehensive illustration of old Bermuda architecture and furnishings. Among the most highly valued exhibits: antique cedar furniture, silverware by Bermuda silversmiths, old English and American pewter, documents and paintings.

Around the corner, a replica of a Gutenberg-era printing press may be seen in the Featherbed Alley Print Shop. The press is in working order. On another little street called Printer's Alley you'll find the **Old Rectory,** a snug timber-and-stone house built in 1705. It's still inhabited.

And so to Bermuda's zealously preserved **St. Peter's Church,** witness to so much of the colony's history, both religious and civic. They've taken no chances with this venerable treasure house: overhead, a battery of modern sprinklers

defends the old cedar beams from the threat of fire.

The first church on this site, roofed with thatched palmetto leaves, was in service in 1612. Improvements and expansion followed over the centuries, starting with the first permanent structure of 1619. The original timbers were often reused in renovations. But the oldest object in the church was an antique even when the early settlers brought it here: a stone font which was used before the era of Columbus.

There are so many historic items worth pointing out in this church that a guide is on duty to help. Don't fail to see the three-tiered pulpit, the bishop's throne said to have been salvaged from a shipwreck, and the area where the colony's first court and first parliament met. In the vestry, take a look at St. George's Chalice, a silver vessel dated 1625–6 and still in regular use. All around the interior walls, dozens of brass or marble memorials, some quite moving, are dedicated to soldiers and statesmen and their loved ones. The most tragic plaque, rather hidden behind the or-

gan near the church entrance, honors the memory of 274 officers, soldiers and dependents (nine of them by name, the rest by rank) of the 56th Regiment. All died here in a lightning epidemic of yellow fever in 1853.

The **churchyard**, where the tombstones tell of epidemics, shipwrecks and war, is well worth a browse. Notice the stone erected by the parents of Midshipman Dale of the United States Navy, wounded and taken prisoner off Bermuda in the War of 1812. Despite the best care he died of his injuries. The inscription thanks the inhabitants of St. George's who gave "the kindest attentions to their son while living and honored him when dead". A memorial salvo is fired over the grave every year to mark U.S.-Bermuda friendship. Other monuments here tell many poignant stories, none more terse and bleak than that conveyed by the twin gravestones of Governor Sir Richard Sharples and his aide, Capt. Hugh Sayers, murdered March 10, 1973.

An early 18th-century limestone house, the **President Henry Tucker House** on Water Street, is run as a museum by the ubiquitous Bermuda National Trust. The "presi-

St. George's Town: Bermudians are welcoming, there's plenty to see.

dent" in the title refers to Henry Tucker's position on the Bermuda Governor's Council at the time of the American Revolution. The house is furnished with valuable 18th-century furniture from Bermuda, America and England. The room that began as a detached kitchen but is now attached to the main house has been turned into a memorial to Joseph Hayne Rainey, who once ran a barber shop on the premises. After the American Civil War, Rainey abandoned his razor and clippers and returned to his native South Carolina, where he was elected as the first black member of the U.S. House of Representatives.

An off-beat museum forms part of the new Somers' Wharf shopping area. The **Carriage Museum** preserves memories of a leisurely Bermuda that was doomed by the legalization of automobiles in 1946. The collection of well-kept carriages—from a dog cart to a brake meant to be propelled by four horses—shows the variety of vehicles driven on the islands' roads until recent times. The names alone stir the imagination: the Victoria, the barouche, the brougham and the semi-formal phaeton.

You'll want to stroll through the tasteful **Somers' Wharf**

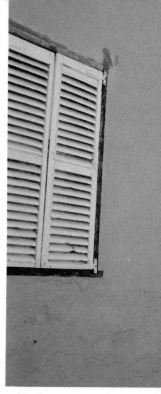

redevelopment project, inspecting the shops and ships. This place has come a long way since the days of smugglers and blockade-runners.

The American Civil War transformed St. George's into a boom town—an offshore supply base for the blockaded South. The Confederate States

Historic streets in St. George's, the first capital of the colony.

set up a combined procurement center and diplomatic and intelligence outpost in the old Globe Hotel. The building has become the **Confederate Museum,** run by the Bermuda National Trust. On show are reminders of the colony's role in helping to arm the South, and of the Confederacy's struggle in general. A replica of the Great Seal of the Confederacy is fitted to a press of the era, so visitors can emboss the symbol of the lost cause in tinfoil or paper.

St. George's Island

There's no end to the historic sights on St. George's Island, and relics of the past crop up everywhere—even on the grounds of a big resort hotel, overlooking the northernmost point of Bermuda. Other hotels claim to be totally self-contained, but the **Club Med** at St. George's Cove even has some ramparts of an old fort, along with the customary swimming pools, tennis courts, shopping arcade and night club. The hotel is surrounded by an executive golf course and there's a private beach down the hill.

Monstrous coast artillery guns, still riding their aiming tracks, stare out from the embrasures of **Fort St. Catherine.** This solid stronghold—some stone walls are eight feet thick —took shape in the 19th century on the site of a wooden fort completed in 1614. Just below the fort is the beach where the *Sea Venture* castaways came ashore five years earlier. Guides in dress uniforms of the mid-19th century show visitors around Fort St. Catherine's battlements and into the labyrinths (fortunately, well lighted) where defenders could have survived a siege that never came. Inside the fort a curious combina-

tion of mementoes may be seen: old flintlocks, replicas of the British crown jewels, cedar carvings by Boer War prisoners, regimental banners of the Commonwealth, and busts of Churchill, Lord Nelson and the Duke of Wellington. Elsewhere in the fort a series of illuminated dioramas illustrate dramatic episodes from Bermuda's history.

One of those incidents was the notorious Gunpowder Plot of August 1775. Under the very noses of His Majesty's forces, a whopping hoard of ammunition was taken from the St. George's magazine, on the grounds of what was then Government House. One hundred kegs of gunpowder were rolled down the hill to Tobacco Bay and quietly ferried out to an American frigate lurking offshore. Tradition has it that the Bermuda ammo assured George Washington's rebel forces their subsequent victory over the British at Boston. More than 300 years later, **Tobacco Bay** shows no sign of treachery or scandal. The beach, less than half a mile west of Fort St. Catherine, is just a flawless rim of sand at the edge of a lazy lagoon.

More forts, some still in use into the 20th century, guard this northern extremity of the colony. Military history fans won't want to miss any of them—the 19th-century Alexandra Battery or Fort Albert, or the 17th-century outpost, **Gates Fort.** You only have to look out from Gates Fort to realize its significance, for this pleasantly landscaped installation is set right alongside the narrow Town Cut channel linking St. George's Harbour with the open sea.

From here you can also look across to PAGET ISLAND, which blocks most of the harbor entrance, with the remains of a vast fort built during the Victorian era. During World War II it was a detention center for enemy aliens.

Beyond Paget, just off the shore of the Naval Air Station, the harbor island called Smith's once served as the repository of Bermuda civilization. From 1610 to 1612 only three men and a dog inhabited the colony. While waiting for new settlers to arrive from England, all three "Kings of Bermuda" chose to live on tiny SMITH'S ISLAND, fishing, hunting and farming. At the start of Bermuda's long history they worked hard to make the most of what they found, and they prospered in their isolation… an apt preamble for what came after.

What to Do

Sports

Although it may look like a floating golf course—the islands boast more golf per square mile than just about anywhere in the world—Bermuda hasn't stinted on other sports. There are close to 100 tennis courts, plus riding trails, stadiums, swimming pools and, of course, beaches to sigh about. Offshore it gets really interesting for fishermen, boatsmen and divers.

Water Sports

Swimming in the aquamarine sea is one of the first things to do; let the more enterprising activities wait till you unwind. The "official" swimming season—when the locals consider the water warm enough to approach—runs from late May to October. But less delicate bathers make the most of the Atlantic from about mid-March to mid-November.

Most hotels have their own or affiliated beach clubs with all facilities. But don't let inertia keep you from trying some of the 30 public beaches, magnificent as Horseshoe Bay or as secluded as Jobson's Cove.

Few perils await Bermuda swimmers, but never forget you're in the Atlantic Ocean. Among the seaborne pests to avoid are so-called red sponge and Portuguese men-of-war (real stingers!), and don't put your foot down on a prickly black sea urchin. Through no fault of its own, Bermuda receives about 100 tons of tar a year. When it washes ashore, clean-up measures are fast and effective, but if your luck runs out, look for a bottle of solvent.

Most hotels also have salt- or fresh-water pools or both.

Snorkeling. You can rent snorkel, mask and flippers at

beach clubs, some shops and hotels. Bermuda's incredibly clear waters, with visibility up to 200 feet ahead, teem with the most stunning fish; anywhere there's a rock there's likely to be a feast for the eyes. For an intimate look at the life of the coral reefs, boat excursions for snorkelers go to the most colorful places, with equipment and expertise all in the package.

Scuba Diving. The winning combination of transparent water, coral reefs and wrecks galore makes Bermuda a most gratifying base for scuba divers. There are introductory courses which start in a swimming pool and work their way down to a deep-sea dive. For divers experienced in the use of self-contained underwater breathing apparatus, excursions go to reefs and wrecks. Treasure hunters will have to compete with some noted local divers, who know more about the legendary 365 Bermuda wrecks than they're telling. But even the "standard", accessible wrecks are exciting to explore. Aside from all the essential equipment you can rent an underwater camera to record your discoveries.

Helmet diving. For non-swimmers, or those who don't dive for fear of getting their hair wet, an entrepreneur at Flatts Village runs helmet-diving expeditions. With a hose feeding air into the big, glass-fronted helmet and a guide leading the way, wide-eyed visitors walk on the ocean floor among the growing coral and doubtless puzzled fish. (For the more sedentary there are many glass-bottom boat tours to the coral gardens.)

Other Water Sports

Fishing is best from May through November. To hear the oldtimers tell it, the only problems here are finding someone to cook your tuna steaks, and engaging the taxidermist to immortalize the big marlin or amberjack you want to hang over the fireplace. Real life may not always deliver the goods, as any fisherman knows, but chances are favorable for hefty catches around Bermuda.

For shore fishing light tackle can be rented by the day. Charter boats go out for reef and deep-sea fishing by the half day and full day, with tackle and bait included. The Bermuda Fishing Information Bureau issues comprehensive booklets (available from Department of Tourism offices) telling everything you need to know, from how to

"chum"—luring otherwise reluctant fish with a free meal—to when and where to find wahoos. They also cover those little diplomatic problems of charter fishing, like how much of the catch the captain keeps and what to tip the mate.

Briefly, anglers who never leave the beach can look forward to meeting bonefish, great barracuda and gray snapper. Reef fishermen drop names like yellowtail snapper, little tunny (bonito), rockfish and grouper. If you go as far as Challenger Bank or Argus Bank, southwest of Bermuda, you'll enter the realm of marlin, swordfish, wahoo, tuna,

Take on the currents of Flatt's Inlet or tee off on one of Bermuda's famed championship courses.

shark and dolphin (the brilliantly colored fish, not the lovable mammal of the same name, alias porpoise).

The annual Bermuda Game Fishing Tournament runs from May 1 to November 30; all visiting and local amateur anglers are eligible to compete for trophies.

Sailing and boating. One of the world's great sailing events, the Newport–Bermuda Ocean Yacht Race, electrifies the islands every other June (in the even-numbered years). Less glamorous races take over Great Sound many weekends. And on certain Sundays you can see the indigenous daredevil racing craft, the Bermuda fitted dinghies (whose crews include bailers).

Boats of many varieties may be rented at marinas around the islands: rowboats or 14-foot Sunfish to play around in, or great sloops that must be professionally crewed. Small motorboats are also available, with or without a captain.

Water-skiing. If you do hire a motorboat, you mustn't use it for skiing without a licensed skipper at the wheel. But hotels can arrange water-ski outings, equipment and instruction included.

Board-skiing. Otherwise known as windsurfing, this California invention has become an Olympic event. Surfboard sails add their dash and color to the Bermuda scene,

too. You can rent one by the hour, or if you need some confidence-building, lessons are available at the same time.

Sports Ashore

Golf. Bermuda is a year-round bonanza for golfers in search of new challenges. You'll need your whole bag of clubs—and tricks—for there's never a dull moment. No two fairways are alike, and the distractions will take your breath away: not the din of freeway traffic or the pressure of duffers piling up behind you at the tee, but million-dollar vistas of the Atlantic framed by flowering hedges and whispering pines. And if you thought Bermuda was completely flat, you're in for some rugged and hilly surprises.

A couple of Bermuda's championship courses are world famous, but all are engrossing. Several hotels have courses on their own grounds. All hotels and guest houses can arrange an introduction to the club you'd like to play. Be sure to have them phone ahead to set the starting time. Wherever you play you won't have far to go to the first tee. Travel agents have informa-

tion on package deals for golfers offered by a number of Bermuda hotels big and small.

Taking a glance at the clubs, from west to east:

Port Royal Golf Course (Southampton parish): 6,411 yards, par 71. Government-owned and open to the public, this Robert Trent Jones course dates from 1970. A couple of fairways cling to clifftops over the Atlantic, adding thrills to some impressively serious golf.

Princess Golf Club (Southampton parish): 2,684 yards, par 54 executive course. The Gibb's Hill lighthouse overhead is only one of the sights on this 18-hole par-three course alongside the Southampton Princess Hotel.

Riddell's Bay Golf and Country Club (Warwick parish): 5,414 yards, par 68. Hilly and windy with narrow fairways; the first hole—418 yards, par four—is Bermuda's toughest starter.

Belmont Hotel, Golf & Beach Club (Warwick parish): 5,777 yards, par 70. All very testing, with tight fairways, elevated greens, blind second shots and headwinds on steep headlands.

Ocean View Golf & Country Club (Devonshire parish): nine holes, 2,956 yards, par 35.

Government owned and open to the public. Ocean View, formerly Queen's Park, is smack in the center of the colony, overlooking the north coast.

Mid Ocean Club (Tucker's Town): 6,547 yards, par 71. The name springs to mind when the pros discuss the greatest golf courses in the world. With its big greens and awesome obstacles, this is Bermuda's longest and most thrillingly beautiful course. Homerun king Babe Ruth couldn't clear Mangrove Lake, the big wet problem on the 5th hole; he lost 11 balls.

Castle Harbour Golf Club (Hamilton parish): 6,445 yards, par 71. Like Mid-Ocean, its next-door neighbor, Castle Harbour shows the skill of Robert Trent Jones. From the elevated first tee, the panorama of green land, blue-green harbor and dark blue sea stirs the heart; at only 312 yards, this par-four starts the day with confidence. But beautiful complications quickly follow.

St. George's Golf Club (St. George's parish): 18 holes, 4,502 yards, par 68. It adjoins the Club Med St. George's Cove village, overlooking Fort St. Catherine.

Tennis. Ardent tennis fans should investigate the special tennis package holidays offered by a few Bermuda hotels. Many other hotels also have courts and pros on the premises. Local courts, many floodlighted, come in a variety of traditional and contemporary surfaces—clay or asphalt, Vynatex or Dynaturf. Note that most places require players to wear proper tennis costumes. The hotel with the biggest tennis complex, the Southampton Princess, has 11 Plexipave courts. Aside from hotels and clubs, there are clay and asphalt courts for day and night play at the Government Tennis Stadium in Bernard Park, just north of Hamilton near Black Watch Pass.

Horseback riding. The abandoned right-of-way of the old Bermuda Railway and trails along the sea provide charming scenery for riding in Bermuda. The hotels have contacts with local stables. A riding school in Warwick offers instruction, accompanied trail rides and the use of "well-mannered horses".

Sports to Watch

Here's your chance to investigate the mysteries of **cricket,** a British tradition which Bermudians, as well as West Indians, have made their own. It's the 91 only game civilized enough to break for tea. Just remember that there are two teams of eleven players, both wearing the same white trousers and shirts. The two players on the field holding bats belong to one team, all the others to the second, whose object is to remove the batsmen. If you happen to be in Bermuda at Cup Match time, late July or early August, you'll find that cricket has eclipsed all other concerns, including business and industry. And well it might, for the St. George's and Somerset sides only decide the island-wide championship once a year.

The rest of the year soccer is the principal sporting con-

A gentlemanly game of cricket proceeds at a leisurely pace.

cern in Bermuda. League matches are played on Saturday and Sunday afternoons; rugby and field hockey may also be watched on weekends.

Motorcycle racing and scrambling takes place on Coney Island, linked with Main Island just beyond Bailey's Bay.

And international golf and tennis tournaments, regattas, and the Bermuda marathon and 10-kilometer races round out the possibilities.

Shopping

Part of Bermuda's allure is sophisticated shopping at advantageous prices. A tradition of understatement carries over into the salesmanship: friendly, helpful sales personnel hover in the background among tasteful displays of high quality, cosmopolitan merchandise. No pushy duty-free bazaar atmosphere on this island; it's more like London's Bond Street without Value Added Tax.

Of course, one shopper's bargain may be another's dud. It depends on where you come from, what's available and at what price. Try to do your homework so you can spot the real bargains when you get to Bermuda. Incidentally, the price on the tag is definitive: no additional taxes are levied, nor is any haggling involved.

Bermuda's prime shopping area—Front Street in Hamilton—offers an uncluttered hoard of select china, crystal, jewelry, woolens and other luxury imports. The major firms have branches in St. George's, some in Somerset and in the important hotels as well. Though goods from Britain and Europe are the biggest attraction for visiting shoppers, don't overlook the **93** work of Bermuda's artisans. Here's a rundown, in alphabetical order, starting with domestic industry, of prospective "buys".

Bermuda Products

Cedar. Candlesticks, coasters, goblets, lamp stands, letter openers, stylized sailing boats… and aromatic sachets of cedar shavings.

Condiments. The local sherry pepper sauce, hot rum pepper sauce, etc., come in travel packs.

Coral. Local coral and sea shells are protected by law, so Bermuda artisans paint pictures on chunks of imported coral for pendants, necklaces, etc. Beautiful seashells are also acquired from abroad for sale to tourists too rushed to go beachcombing.

Dolls. Since Bermuda has no national costume of its own, dollmakers improvise with flowery Caribbean-style dress; some shops also sell Brazilian dolls with fruity Carmen Miranda hats.

Fashions. Island themes or flowers figure in the cheerful patterns of Bermuda-made scarves, skirts, handbags.

Jewelry. Bermuda motifs distinguish some fine island-crafted jewelry. Artisans here work with gold, silver, precious stones, beads and minute seashells.

Liqueur. The fruit of the loquat tree goes into a strong but sweet liqueur suitable for sipping straight or mixing into tropical drinks.

Maps and prints. Historic charts of Bermuda and similar memorabilia, in frameable reproductions.

Marmalade. The small but delicious Bermuda citrus crop contributes to the success of home-made marmalades.

Perfume. Island flowers, distilled into scent, make a long-lasting reminder of Bermuda. Note, too, major bargains in French perfumes.

Pottery. Souvenir mugs and plates; hand-thrown miniature pots, plates and jugs; figurines.

Records and tapes. Instant memories of calypso and steelband music by Bermuda's own groups.

Sand. Yes, they even bottle pink Bermuda sand so you can impress friends at home.

Stamps and coins. Bermuda's pretty postage stamps are collectors' items; numismatists look to island dealers for valuable local and foreign coins.

Steel drums. Unless you're really crazy about steelband music, the best bet is a *miniature* of the tropical instrument.

Straw goods. Bags, hats and knickknacks, hand-plaited.

Toiletries. Soap and after-shave in spicy Bermuda fragrances.

Watercolors, oils, prints. Bermudian artists are prolific, especially with seascapes and studies of flowers.

Street vendors sell fresh fruit and vegetables the old-fashioned way.

Imported Goods

Antiques. Mostly British curios, old boxes, toys, plates; period furniture and silver for very serious collectors. Bermuda-made antiques are extremely rare on the market.

Cameras and accessories. Be sure to check out the cost of Japanese and German gear at home and compare prices before you decide; bargains can be found in Bermuda.

China. Minton, Rosenthal, Royal Copenhagen, Spode and Wedgwood are among the big-name attractions for Bermuda bargain hunters.

Cigars. Connoisseurs covet the expensive hand-rolled Cuban classics sold in Bermuda, but beware U.S. customs complications. Note that tobacco for consumption on the island **95**

is no bargain, but export packs are available for plane or ship.

Crystal. Look for fine Irish, French and other European crystal at favorable prices.

Fashions for women. Beachwear, pants suits, sportswear, silk scarves and blouses.

Figurines. Lladro from Spain, Hummel from Germany and lesser-known ceramic character studies.

Liquor. Duty-free prices available only on five-bottle packs purchased in advance,

delivered to the airport or aboard ship. Infinite combinations of Scottish, Canadian, American, European spirits or Bermuda-blended rum. Note customs charges for Americans.

Sweaters. Fisherman's, classic, or high-fashion styles. Mostly Irish and Scottish, in a warming range of styles, colors and sizes. Among the all-time favorites of Bermuda shoppers.

Tea. Gift packages of traditional English blends.

Watches and clocks. Many brand names and models from Japan and Switzerland. Do some comparison-shopping before you leave home.

From flowers to fragrance; the scent of the islands is distilled in a long and painstaking process.

Nightlife

Just about everyone—jet-setters, inexhaustible rockers, and people who don't go to nightclubs at home—will enjoy nights out in Bermuda. From elaborate production numbers in hotel nightclubs to beery old songs in a pub, entertainment matches many tastes and moods.

The major resort hotels schedule nightly festivities combining live dance music, a variety show of local performers and perhaps an imported "name" act. Local talent specializes in the Bermudian version of West Indian traditions like fiery, acrobatic limbo dancing, steelband music and calypso. Listen closely to the words of the calypso songs, strong on risqué double meaning and topical political themes. If you've never heard the subtlety and versatility of steelband music you're due for a lilting surprise.

Beyond the hotels are a number of nightclubs and discos, mostly in or near Hamilton. They have dancing and variety shows, or just dancing and more dancing. The discos fiercely compete for the most novel sound and light effects.

Quieter entertainment goes on in some smaller hotels, cot-

You can dance the night away in one of Hamilton's lively discos.

tage colonies and pub-restaurants—a singer or two, a small combo, or a piano tinkling romantic favorites. Or you can just find a friendly pub where **97** the nightly dart competition proves the height of excitement.

And if you haven't just stepped off a cruise liner you can change the pace by signing up for one of the moonlight cruises in Great Sound with "dancing under the stars".

To find out what's on, check the weekly calendars in the free brochures distributed at hotels and the tourist office, and the ads in the newspapers. Reservations are often essen-tial, always advisable. As for dress, propriety is stressed; unless otherwise advertised, clubs require men to wear jackets, with ties "suggested". Some places have cover charges, others a minimum, and still others an all-in charge including a couple of drinks and gratuities.

In season, the colony's top hotels feature star-studded nightclub acts and non-stop entertainment.

Some Festivals and Special Events

December–March   *Bermuda Rendezvous Time.* Special events and hospitality for winter visitors.

January   *Bermuda International Marathon and 10-Kilometer Race.* Both visitors and residents can compete.

January–February   *Bermuda Festival.* Five lively weeks of jazz, opera, concerts, drama, including some renowned performers.

March–April   *Bermuda College Weeks.* Free parties, cruises and entertainment cleverly lure vacationing college students to the islands; they usually return for honeymoons, anniversaries, etc.

March–May   *Homes and Gardens Tours.* Visits take place every Wednesday; sponsored by the Garden Club of Bermuda.

April   *Peppercorn Ceremony.* The governor, in all his colonial finery, accepts one peppercorn ostentatiously paid as rent for the 17th-century Old State House building, St. George's.

May   *Bermuda Day.* Folkloric floats on parade; opening of beach season.

June   *Queen's Birthday.* Bermuda Regiment parades down Front Street, Hamilton, and the governor accepts the salute.

June (alternate years)   *Newport-Bermuda Yacht Race.* Beautiful ocean-crossing yachts and parties galore.

July or August   *Cup Match.* Classic two-day struggle for Bermuda's cricket championship.

October   *Convening of Parliament.* Resplendent uniforms and British pomp.

December 26   *Boxing Day.* Public holiday saluted by Gombey dancers, in grotesque masks and costumes, with drumpowered rituals largely of African derivation.

Dining Out

For a small island in mid-ocean, Bermuda acquits itself well in the wining-and-dining department. International gourmets won't quibble over the new-wave French cooking or the wine cellars. Gastronomic adventurers have a chance to test ingenious native recipes. Conservatives homesick for hamburgers, pizza or fish and chips need suffer no withdrawal pains. Bermuda's many restaurants run the gamut from candlelit *haute cuisine* to the most down-to-earth cafés. The prices, too, vary from daunting to moderate.

Lunch is usually served from noon to 2.30 or 3 p.m. Dinner begins anytime after 6.30 or 7 p.m., later in the more elegant places. It's wise to reserve a table at any good restaurant for lunch or dinner. The tipping problem is solved in many establishments which automatically add 15 percent to the bill, but be sure to ascertain the situation.

Breakfast
Hotels serve breakfast from about 8 to 10 a.m.—in your room, on your balcony, around the pool or in the hotel restaurant. Some meal plans provide a slightly spartan continental breakfast, others lay on juice, bacon and eggs, toast and jam with your pot of coffee or tea. On Sunday some hotels set up an enterprising brunch starting about noon, a smorgasbord affair with a plethora of hot and cold dishes to choose from.

For a drastic change of pace you might try the traditional Bermuda Sunday breakfast: boiled salt codfish with tomato and onion sauce, boiled potatoes, hard-boiled egg—and a banana on the side. It tastes like a compromise between Portuguese and Caribbean cooking, but it's really Bermuda's own.

Soups
Bermuda fish chowder, a rousing way to start lunch or dinner, is a highly spiced thick broth usually served with a dash of sherry or rum and a squeeze of lemon. Beyond the principal ingredient, fish heads, the cook employs fresh fish, onions, celery, salt pork tomatoes and a garden of herbs.

Conch chowder is another Bermuda favorite, although the main ingredient is usually imported. Aside from the mollusks it contains celery, onion, tomatoes. potato, salt pork, herbs and perhaps a dash of cream.

Portuguese red bean soup, another Bermuda standby, sometimes comes as thick and spicy as Texas chili con carne. It's certainly a he-man soup, with kidney beans, potato, tomato, onion, garlic, kale, and chunks of ham and sausage.

More sophisticated restaurants broaden the soup repertoire with French onion soup, chilled vichyssoise, gazpacho and cream of avocado soup.

Fish and Seafood

If you want fresh local fish, be sure to ask what's available. Bermuda red snapper, rockfish, wahoo or tuna steak— or lobster in season—can't be beat. However, much of the seafood served on the islands is habitually imported—giant shrimps, scallops, Dover sole and crab, for instance.

The monarch of shellfish in Bermuda waters is the spiny lobster, similar to cold-water lobsters except that it lacks bit-

ing claws. When the local supply is insufficient, lobster from Maine sometimes appears on menus. The season is September through March. Lobster is served broiled with melted butter, baked in a Thermidor cheese sauce, or sauteed in chunks with brandy and covered with a cream sauce.

Fresh fish is served broiled or pan-fried or poached in wine sauce or bountifully stuffed and baked. In many cases, fish is filleted as a matter of course.

The resort hotels regale guests with elaborate buffet suppers.

A favorite Bermuda seafood dish, mussel pie, is a slightly curried thick clam stew in a pastry shell. Another island specialty may sound barbarous but tastes rich: Bermuda shark. It reaches the table after several beneficial transformations, arriving in tiny pieces cooked with onions, peppers, parsley, thyme and mustard greens.

Meat and Vegetables
Meat-eaters will find all the familiar cuts and recipes—standard steaks and chops, French-style baby lamb, Italian veal scallopine and chicken cacciatore. The vegetables in-

clude some Bermuda specialties. Between the *asperges à la Hollandaise* and the *pommes de terre variées* on a pretentious menu you're likely to find a startlingly down-home entry, peas'n'rice. In other Bermuda circles this is called Hop'n John, and it's so good it can be stretched into a main dish. Aside from the advertised peas and rice it probably contains a Bermuda onion, bacon or chicken, and a sliced Portuguese sausage. Those famous onions are so tasty they're featured in many a dish, such as onions in cream or onion pie.

Less familiar, perhaps, is the Bermuda pawpaw, known elsewhere as papaya, and used on the island in a double capacity, as a fruit and a vegetable; baked pawpaw comes out as a creamy, cheesy casserole. Pumpkin, plantain and christophene (a kind of squash) are also dressed up for dinner.

Desserts

Half the desserts available carry a suggestion of Olde English abandon, while the others have tropical overtones. Local fruits, fresh or cooked, give a West Indies sweetness to the end of a meal—strawberries, loquats (plum-like, originally from Japan), jumbo grapefruit, watermelon, Surinam cherries, banana fritters.... As for those English sweets, you'll encounter trifle —jelly-roll or sponge cake drowned in sherry and laden with peaches or strawberries, bananas, chopped nuts, custard and whipped cream. By comparison Bermuda syllabub —guava jelly, port or sherry, and whipped cream—sounds suitable for dieters.

Holiday Specials

Cassava pie, a Christmas season specialty, has been a Bermuda favorite for hundreds of years. Cassava, also known as manioc, was imported from the West Indies in the earliest days of the colony. In Bermuda's national dish it is combined with chicken, pork, eggs, and perhaps brandy or sherry in a sweetish but meaty layered pie.

Fireworks are no longer permitted in Bermuda on Guy Fawkes Day (November 5), when the British celebrate the failure of the gunpowder plot of 1605. But sweet potato pudding—a sort of spice cake— remains an essential part of holiday parties on the island. Cinnamon, cloves and lemon or orange juice add counterpoint to the yam's bland sweetness.

Drinks

Before dinner, Bermudians are apt to indulge in a rum drink or two, the most talked about being the Rum Swizzle. Every bartender has his secret recipe, which could be as intricate as this one: light rum, black rum, fruit brandy, lime juice, honey or sugar syrup, and a dash of bitters. With crushed ice added, it's agitated by rubbing a pronged stick between the palms of the hands... hence the expression "swizzle stick", or was it vice-versa?

The aromatic bitters playing a minor role in the swizzle should not be confused with the English beer called bitter, a popular, robust drink day or night. In Bermuda pubs, imported draft bitter is drunk by the pint. Bottled American and other European beers are also available, and so are all the best-known brands of spirits.

With dinner you'll be able to choose from comprehensive wine lists which usually include a reasonably priced carafe. Or choose a soft drink, imported mineral water, fruit punch, or even pure Bermuda rainwater.

Bermuda swizzles are garnished with fruit, fortified with rum.

BLUEPRINT for a Perfect Trip

How to Get There

Airline fares and regulations can be most bewildering, even to seasoned travellers. Always consult a reliable travel agent when planning your holiday, so that you can find the best option for your timetable and budget. The information given below is intended simply as a guideline.

From North America

BY AIR: Bermuda is easily accessible from the major cities in the United States and Canada. There are direct flights from about a dozen U.S. cities, as well as from Toronto, with connecting flights from most other North American centers.

Bermuda is an extremely popular destination, and there are a variety of promotional fares available, dependent on when you want to travel in the year, and also for how long you want to stay. Contact your travel agent for available deals.

Charter Flights and Package Tours: Charter flights to Bermuda are rarely offered. Package tours feature hotel, transfers, a choice of sightseeing and a specific meal plan. The Bermuda week runs for six nights, seven days. Since Bermuda is known for its golf courses and abundant tennis courts as well as for being a destination for honeymooners, packages are available catering to specific needs.

From Great Britain

BY AIR: There are non-stop scheduled flights from London to Bermuda; flying time is about 7 hours. Passengers from the provinces connect with flights from London.

There are first- and club-class fares, plus selected economy fares on flights from London to Bermuda. It is possible to buy cheaper fares, but these are subject to time restrictions. For some of these fares you must book and pay in advance.

Package Tours: There are no charter flights to Bermuda, but there's a wide range of one- and two-week package tours. These must be booked in advance. Prices vary, depending on whether you stay in a hotel or apartment or arrange your own accommodations. It is always wise to take out an insurance so that you are covered if there are any changes in the tour.

When to Go

Bermuda is 1,000 miles north of the West Indies, so it's not the place to choose for ocean swimming in February. However, the winter months in Bermuda are as mild as spring in more northerly regions.

Summery weather can be expected from May to mid-November. It's likely to be hot and humid.

There is no rainy season; precipitation is rather evenly distributed around the calendar—a fortunate feature, for the islanders are heavily dependent on rainwater. The windy season is in winter. The hurricane season is usually late summer and autumn, but Bermuda has rarely borne the full brunt of these tropical cyclones which afflict the Caribbean area.

Here are some average temperatures to help you guess what to expect in Bermuda:

AIR		J	F	M	A	M	J	J	A	S	O	N	D
Max.	°F	68	68	68	70	75	80	84	85	83	79	74	70
	°C	20	20	20	21	24	27	29	29	28	26	23	21
Min.	°F	60	59	60	60	66	73	75	76	75	72	67	62
	°C	16	15	15	16	19	23	24	25	24	22	20	17

Planning Your Budget

To give you an idea of what to expect, here's a sampling of average prices a visitor is likely to encounter in Bermuda.

Accommodations (double room per person per night). *Luxury hotel* (MAP): high season $127–200, low season $115. *Small hotel* (MAP): high season $100–140, low season $95. *Guest houses:* high season $40–50, low season $40. Add service charge.

Admissions. Aquarium $4, Maritime Museum $5, Crystal Caves $3.

Airport departure tax. $15.

Bicycle and moped rental. *Bicycles:* $10 per day, $35 per week. *Mopeds:* single-seater $20 per day, $71 for 4 days, add $20 deposit; double-seater $36 per day, $127 for 4 days, add $20 deposit.

Buses. Hamilton to Botanical Gardens $1.25, Somerset to St. George's $2.50.

Carriages. Single (2 persons) $15 per half-hour, double (4 persons) $20.

Cigarettes. Packs of 20 American with filter $3.25.

Dry cleaning. Jacket $6.50, dress $9, skirt $6.50.

Entertainment. Nightclub cover charge $7–15, movie $6.

Ferries. Hamilton to Paget $1, to Somerset $2.

Guided tours. $20 per hour for 4-seater, $30 per hour for 6-seater, 3-hour water tour $20 per person.

Hairdressers. *Woman's* wash and cut $40, wash and blow-dry $23. *Man's* wash and cut $17.

Meals and drinks. Pub lunch $7, dinner (good establishment) $40, bottle of wine $17, carafe $10, beer $3.

Sports. *Golf:* green fees $25. *Sailing:* sunfish $20 per hour, $80 per day. *Waterskiing:* $50 per half-hour, $85 per hour. *Sailboards:* $15–20 per hour. *Parasailing:* $33 per half-hour.

Taxis. Airport to Hamilton approx. $16, Hamilton to South Shore $15, Somerset to St. George's $30.

An A–Z Summary of Practical Information and Facts

A star (*) following a entry indicates that relevant prices are to be found on page 108.

ACCOMMODATIONS*. Bermuda offers a broad range of accommodations, from resort hotels as lavish as any in the world to simple guest houses. However, the number of rooms in the top bracket far exceeds the availabilities in the economy class.

The Bermuda Department of Tourism issues a comprehensive booklet, *Where to Stay in Bermuda*, listing every one of the island's registered hotels, cottage complexes, etc., including a picture of each place with some details of facilities and atmosphere. A supplementary bulletin gives the rates for each establishment—but note that tax and service charges are added.

Hotels and guest houses of all classes have reduced rates in winter—from November or December to the end of February or mid-March. But the Department of Tourism points out that entertainment and facilities may be cut back during this season.

Disabled visitors should ask for the pamphlet *Access to Bermuda*, issued by the local chapter of the Society for the Advancement of Travel for the Handicapped. This lists accommodations offering facilities for wheelchairs, as well as accessible tourist attractions and restaurants.

Visitors are always urged to book early for Bermuda through authorized travel agents.

Hotels usually offer a choice between two meal plans, abbreviated MAP and BP. MAP, Modified American Plan, includes breakfast and dinner in the price of the room. plus in some places British-style afternoon tea. BP, Bermuda Plan. covers room and full breakfast only. Housekeeping cottages and guest houses (see below) may offer Bermuda Plan or a slightly stripped-down CP (Continental Plan), room and light breakfast, or EP (European Plan), room only. Visitors who choose the non-American plans will find no shortage of restaurants of all varieties on the island.

The big hotels and many of the smaller establishments advertise special package holidays for honeymooners, golfers, tennis fans and

A other special-interest visitors. These usually include extra activities or facilities at little or no additional cost.

Most of the large hotels have shopping arcades, bars, nightclubs, restaurants, tennis courts and swimming pools on the premises. Some have their own private beaches; others send their guests to associated beach clubs. The big hotels either have their own golf courses or offer their guests privileges at nearby clubs.

The smaller hotels have limited on-site facilities for shopping and entertainment and are less formal.

Cottage colonies, a Bermudian idea, disperse the living quarters through spacious grounds, with a main clubhouse, dining room and bar for the gregarious. All have their own beaches or pools but limited entertainment. Cottage colonies can be very luxurious.

Bermuda also has two exclusive **club resorts** noted for privacy and luxury. You have to be a member, or be introduced by a member, to get a reservation.

Turning to more economical facilities, the Bermuda equivalent of "efficiency units" or "service flats" are called **housekeeping cottages and apartments.** These are arranged in dispersed cottages or small apartment houses, usually in roomy surroundings with a pool or beach or both. Budget-conscious visitors appreciate the kitchenettes for cutting down on restaurant bills.

Guest houses, the least expensive of all, range from old mansions with spacious accommodations to more modest private houses with smaller rooms and even less formality. Some serve breakfast and a few offer an advantageous Modified American Plan to include home-cooked dinners. And some have housekeeping units or shared kitchen facilities.

AIRPORT. Commercial aircraft and military planes alike use the facilities of the United States Naval Air Station at the east end of Bermuda. The Civil Air Terminal, a white two-storied building, has a Bermudian feeling—from the smiles of the immigration inspectors to the potted semitropical plants brightening the baggage claim area. The Arrivals area is often crowded around midday, when most flights from the U.S. arrive in quick succession.

After immigration formalities and customs inspection, arriving passengers head for their hotels. But first there are maps and brochures to be picked up at the Visitors Service Bureau desk. A branch bank is available if you want to cash a traveler's check, but you won't need **110** Bermudian money to pay the taxi; U.S. currency is completely interchangeable with Bermudian money here. Porters are on duty to take your baggage out to the taxi stand or the departure point for limousines going to the hotels. Taxis take 20–30 minutes to Hamilton and central parishes.

Outbound: On your way home, ask your hotel receptionist to arrange a taxi or limousine pickup for the airport. Check-in is 75 minutes before departure on services to the United States. This is to allow time to pass through U.S. Customs *before* leaving the island (it's wise to fill out the declaration form—available at hotels and airlines—before going to the airport). There is no duty-free shop at the airport. Passengers who have previously ordered duty-free goods from island stores should show the sales slips to the U.S. Customs agent, then pick up the purchases before boarding the plane.

BICYCLE and MOPED RENTAL*. See also box, p. 46. "Auxiliary cycles" or "livery cycles", as the Bermudians call them, are mopeds ideally suited to an island of this size with a 20-mile-an-hour speed limit. Visitors need no license to hire and drive them. It's relatively easy to learn to operate the automatic gearshift, and free instruction is always offered.

There are two principal categories of auxiliary cycle: the smaller, cheaper type is essentially a bicycle with an auxiliary motor which can't climb a steep hill without the help of the pedals. The more powerful (and more expensive) mopeds have all the power it takes to conquer any of Bermuda's hills and would be quite capable of speeds above the local limit. Included in the rental fee is a crash helmet, the use of which is compulsory. You may be asked to leave a deposit and to pay in advance.

Old-fashioned pedal bicycles, called "push bikes" here, are also available, for perhaps one-third the price of a moped. There are one-speed, three-, five- and ten-speed models for rent, and many pleasant byways to explore. But the rush hour in the Hamilton area is anything but relaxed; and the hilly terrain will seem more challenging than you first thought.

Remember to drive on the left!

CAMPING. Bermuda residents are permitted to camp in certain areas of the islands, but visitors traveling independently may not. Space at certain sites may, however, be reserved for organized groups.

CAR RENTAL. Visitors may not rent cars in Bermuda. See Transportation and Bicycle and Moped Rental.

C **CHILDREN.** Some hotels offer special rates for children, but others exclude them. Be sure to find out in advance.

Babysitters are no problem in the larger hotels, and the charges are not excessive.

Bermuda has many attractions for children: the Aquarium and its children's zoo, St. George's Town with historic sights including stocks and pillory, the Maritime Museum with sunken treasure and historic boats, the various forts, Devil's Hole fish pond and the illuminated caves between Harrington Sound and Castle Harbour. Sports opportunities are also most varied.

CIGARETTES, CIGARS, TOBACCO*. Tobacconists and many other shops stock a wide range of cigarettes, mostly American and British. Prices are high, since "duty-free" considerations do not apply to tobacco products consumed on the island. Specialist shops carry a full line of imported smoking tobacco and classic cigars from Cuba (which Americans can enjoy in Bermuda but not import to the U.S.).

There are some restrictions on smoking in public places, including movie theaters but not buses.

CLOTHING. Decorum is more pronounced in Bermuda than in most resorts; chalk it up to British reserve. Immodest clothing rates censure in hotels and on the streets, and "dressing for dinner" is standard for festive occasions. A famous photo of the 1950s shows a policeman, in Bermuda shorts, applying a tape measure to the exposed leg of a woman in medium-length shorts. If she had bared more than three inches above the knee, the lady would have been warned to cover up. Happily, no such stodginess applies to the beaches, where bikinis fit nicely into the scenery.

During the daytime, the rule is informality but not abandon. Thus bathing suits and bare feet are out of the question in hotel lobbies and on the street. Ladies are specifically barred from wearing hair curlers in public.

At dinner and thereafter, gentlemen are expected to wear jackets and ties in some hotel restaurants and nightclubs. Evening clothes are not normally obligatory, but many people dress up, especially on Saturday nights, in the more elegant places.

A vastly more informal set of rules applies in guest houses and housekeeping cottages, but the same standard of propriety remains for public appearances.

Summer visitors will have little trouble packing: everything should **112** be lightweight. In winter, be sure to have a topcoat or raincoat and a sweater or two, with most of your clothes in the fall-weight category. (But don't forget shorts and swimsuits.) When in doubt, pack less rather than more. Bermuda's shops are famous for their high-quality imported clothing, so you can soon fill any gaps in your wardrobe once you're on the spot.

COMMUNICATIONS

Post offices are found in every parish. They are open from 8 a.m. to 5 p.m. Monday through Friday (the smaller ones close for lunch). The General Post Office at Church and Parliament streets in Hamilton is also open on Saturdays from 8 a.m. until noon.

Mail may be dropped into the British-style red pillar boxes on the streets, with the monogram of Queen Elizabeth II or earlier monarchs.

If you're uncertain of your address in Bermuda you may have mail sent to you c/o General Delivery, Hamilton, Bermuda. Letters may be picked up at the General Delivery window in the General Post Office.

Though letters and postcards sent at surface rates normally go to and from Bermuda by air, those marked for airmail and with the correct postage take priority in the airlift.

Telegrams and Telex. Cable and Wireless Ltd. operates Bermuda's international telecommunications system, offering comprehensive and efficient worldwide service. Cablegrams may be sent from the company's main office, opposite the City Hall in Hamilton. Cable and Wireless also provides instantaneous worldwide telex communications, as well as specialized services for business and maritime interests.

Telephone. Cable and Wireless also handles Bermuda's international telephone service. Bermuda subscribers can direct-dial calls to the U.S., Canada, Britain and many other countries. From any public telephone in Bermuda you can make a credit-card or collect call to any country which accepts such calls. To reach the international operator, dial 0.

Bermuda's domestic telephone system, more than a century old, is run on the most modern standards by the Bermuda Telephone Company Ltd. In terms of the number of telephones per capita, Bermuda ranks among the world's most advanced nations. There are hundreds of public telephones in booths on the streets and in public places. To make a local call, be sure to follow the printed instructions (which can vary): wait for the dial tone, dial the number, then wait until the party has answered before depositing the coin. For information, dial 902.

C **COMPLAINTS.** Your first move, clearly, would be to complain to the manager of the offending store, restaurant or hotel. But if this fails to give satisfaction, take your problem to the Bermuda Department of Tourism. Their main office is at Global House, Church Street, Hamilton.

CONSULATES. The Consulate General of the United States is at "Crown Hill" on Middle Road in Devonshire, just outside Hamilton; tel. 295-1342.

The only other country maintaining full consular service in Bermuda is Portugal (Melbourne House, 11 Parliament Street, Hamilton).
Countries served by Honorary Consuls include Belgium, Denmark, Finland, France, the Netherlands, Norway and Sweden. For addresses and telephone numbers look in the telephone directory under "Consular Representation".

CONVERTER CHARTS. Bermuda is in the process of converting from Imperial measures to the metric system used in most of the rest of the world. Thus fuel is now sold in liters, distance signs are expressed in kilometers instead of miles, and the weather reports on the radio cite both the Fahrenheit and Celsius readings. Traditionalists refuse to let them change the measure of a pint of beer (.568 liter).

Temperature

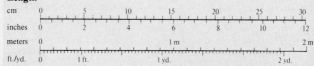

Length

Distance

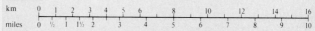

Weight

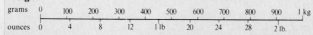

Fluid measures

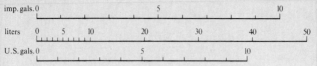

CRIME and THEFT. Bermuda's police blotter shows an increasing incidence of petty crime, so reasonable precautions are indicated. If you must bring valuable jewelry with you, be sure to store it in the hotel safe. Don't leave your property unattended on the beach. If you rent a bike or moped be sure to lock it when you park, and leave it in a well-lit place at night.

Don't risk becoming a criminal yourself. Bermuda deals severely with anyone caught importing or possessing "unlawful drugs", including marijuana. Firearms and ammunition may not be imported—and that prohibition covers underwater spearguns as well. In 1980, the law was expanded to cover crossbows, flick-knives, blowguns and other bizarre instruments.

CUSTOMS and ENTRY REGULATIONS. See also AIRPORT and CRIME AND THEFT. No visa is required by Americans, Britons or citizens of the Irish Republic, Australia and New Zealand. South Africans (among other nationals) need one, unless they are permanent residents of the U.S. or Canada. All visitors to Bermuda must have a valid passport. An exception is made for citizens of the U.S. or Canada, who need only show proof of citizenship or nationality. All visitors entering Bermuda must hold a ticket for return or onward travel to a country where they have current right of entry.

Smallpox vaccination certificates are no longer required, except in the case of travelers who have been in an infected country within the preceding two weeks.

"Bona fide visitors" may remain in Bermuda for up to three weeks. If you wish to stay longer, you have to apply in person to the Department of Immigration in the Government Administration Building, on Parliament Street, Hamilton. For those who wish to live or work in Bermuda, permission must be applied for in advance.

The chart on the following page shows what main duty-free items you may take into Bermuda and, when returning home, into your own country:

C

Into:	Cigarettes		Cigars		Tobacco	Spirits		Wine
Bermuda	200	and	50	and	454 g.	1.1 l.	and	1.1 l.
Canada*	200	and	50	and	908 g.	1.1 l.	or	1.1 l.
U.K.	200	or	50	or	250 g.	1 l.	and	2 l.
U.S.A.*	200	and	100	and	**	1 l.	or	1 l.

   * after 48 hours abroad
  ** a reasonable quantity

Currency restrictions. There's no restriction on the amount of foreign money you can bring into or take out of Bermuda providing it's declared upon arrival, but you can only export a maximum of 250 Bermuda dollars.

E **ELECTRIC CURRENT.** Appliances in Bermuda run on the same kind of power as in the U.S. and Canada—110-volt, 60-cycle A.C. The plugs are the same size, too. For visitors from Britain, dual-voltage appliances will need American-size plugs; other electrical appliances are not interchangeable.

EMERGENCIES. Here are the emergency numbers you can dial from any telephone in Bermuda:

Police emergency	911
Fire	911
Ambulance	911
Air-Sea Rescue	297-1010

G **GUIDES*.** Any taxi displaying a small blue flag is driven by a qualified tour guide. There is no provision in Bermuda for foreign-language guides.

H **HAIRDRESSERS and BARBERSHOPS*.** The big resort hotels of Bermuda have hairdressers and barbershops on the premises. Other such establishments, from elegant to spartan, may be found in Hamilton. There are both unisex salons and the more traditional variety of **116** women's hairdressers and men's barbershops.

HEALTH and MEDICAL CARE. See also EMERGENCIES. Bermuda is one island where you can eat the food and drink the water without a care. No special health precautions are indicated except for avoiding too much sun on first exposure. Incidentally, hay fever sufferers find Bermuda a haven, for there is no ragweed (but all those flowers may annoy some other allergies).

In case of illness or accident, you'll be glad to know that Bermuda has a large, well-equipped hospital, the King Edward VII Memorial Hospital, next to the Botanical Gardens. Bermuda has no National Health Service, only private medicine. Be sure your health insurance coverage is up-to-date.

If you must use prescribed drugs, be sure to carry a sufficient supply and show the prescription to the customs inspector when you arrive. (The importation of any drugs which have not been prescribed is forbidden.) Bermuda pharmacists will not fill prescriptions written by overseas doctors.

Pharmacies are found in many locations around the island. While there is no round-the-clock service, one or another of the shops is open from 8 a.m. to 9 p.m. Monday through Saturday, and at various times between 10 a.m. and 6.30 p.m. on Sundays.

HURRICANES. Although Bermuda is off the beaten track for hurricanes, one of these monumental Atlantic storms is liable to strike the island every 20 or 30 years. Defined as a violent storm with winds of more than 75 miles per hour, a hurricane is accompanied by torrential rain and high tides. Thanks to satellite forecasts and weather flights, hurricanes no longer come as a surprise. The meteorologists provide plenty of warning, allowing time for battening the hatches and inviting friends to hurricane parties. The most likely season for a hurricane is autumn, specifically September and October.

LANGUAGE. The language of Bermuda is English, often spoken with a mid-Atlantic accent. Much of the vocabulary is British, as is the spelling, and some Caribbean-sounding slang may be heard. But North Americans need fear no problems of communication.

LAUNDRY and DRY CLEANING*. Hotels provide speedy laundry service, sometimes on a same-day express basis. There are, as well, do-it-yourself laundromats around the island; look in the classified telephone directory under "Laundries" for addresses. For dry cleaning, hotels and commercial cleaners in town return the clothes in 48 hours. **117**

L **LOST and FOUND.** To trace lost or misplaced property in Bermuda, go to the nearest police station.

M **MAPS.** The Bermuda Department of Tourism issues, free, a good map of the island showing major and minor roads, tourist attractions, beaches and hotels, and including town maps of Hamilton and St. George's. Visitors requiring more detail may be interested in what's titled the *Bermuda Tourist Map*, on sale at the Public Works Department, next to the General Post Office on Parliament Street, Hamilton. A detailed 24-page map booklet with index, "Bermuda Islands Guide", is a popular choice and is on sale at most bookshops and drug stores.

MEETING PEOPLE. What with the beaches and the pubs, it's not hard to make new friends in Bermuda. Students traditionally get acquainted during College Weeks in March and April, when the government underwrites a succession of beach parties, boat cruises and the like. Children under the age of 18 can compete against local kids in the golf and tennis tournaments that are held at various times during the year.

Bermudians are famous for their friendliness and welcome visitors to attend meetings of any of the dozens of clubs and organizations that have been founded on the islands. The Department of Tourism will gladly supply you with the names and addresses of such groups as the Rotary Club, English Speaking Union, Bermuda Bridge Club, Sea Shell Club, Croquet Club, etc. Check, too, with the tourist authorities about taking part in a variety of special events like the annual walking tour of Bermuda or the Garden Club's Spring Home and Garden tours. Or sign up to play in a chess, backgammon, tennis or golf tournament. The possibilities are endless.

MONEY MATTERS

Currency. It's all much easier since the traditional pounds, shillings and pence gave way to decimal currency in 1979. And even easier now that the Bermuda dollar is pegged to the U.S. dollar, eliminating conversion tables and furrowed brows. In fact, American currency is interchangeable with Bermuda money on the island; you may get your change in a mixture of local and U.S. bills and coins. (But be sure to convert all your Bermuda money before you leave the island.) Canadian dollars are accepted in some establishments at the latest exchange rate. British and other currencies must be changed in banks.

118 *Banknotes:* $2, 5, 20, 50, 100. *Coins:* 1¢, 5¢, 10¢, 25¢ and $1.

Coins are the same size as their American equivalents, with the profile of Queen Elizabeth II on the front and symbolic island designs on the reverse side.

For currency restrictions, see CUSTOMS AND ENTRY REGULATIONS.

Banks. Bermuda's four banks, and their branch offices, are open from 9:30 a.m. to 3 p.m. Monday through Friday, with an extra hour for late business from 4:30 to 5:30 p.m. every Friday. Although this is a small, isolated island, the banks are geared for all manner of sophisticated international transactions.

Traveler's checks. In U.S. dollar denominations, traveler's checks are accepted everywhere. The banks can handle them in all other currencies.

Credit cards. Well-known international credit cards are accepted in many shops and restaurants, and most of the big hotels, but not in smaller hotels, cottages and guest houses.

NEWSPAPERS and MAGAZINES. Bermuda's daily newspaper, *The Royal Gazette,* covers local affairs in detail along with a quota of international news. For different angles on the local scene there are two weeklies, the *Mid-Ocean News, The Bermuda Sun,* and *The Bermuda Times.*

Newspapers from overseas arrive regularly by air. The major dailies from Boston, New York, Philadelphia and Washington, as well as leading Canadian papers, are on sale late on the day of publication. A wide selection of British newspapers is also available the same day they appear. The fat American Sunday papers go on sale at 5 p.m., their prices significantly inflated by the air-freight charges.

PARKS. Bermuda is dotted with parks and public gardens, in the towns and in the country. Among the highspots: Par-la-Ville Gardens, in the center of Hamilton, is the handiest place to escape the bustle of the capital. Skilful planning and transplanting keeps the hilly park in bloom all the time. Elsewhere in the town, Victoria Park has tall shady trees, flower beds and a 19th-century bandstand.

In St. George's, distinguished palm trees stand out above Somers Gardens, commemorating Sir George Somers, the founder of the colony. He left his heart here, literally; it's buried in the park.

Some of the biggest parks surround the island's historic forts. Fort Hamilton, overlooking the capital and the harbor, includes a rare tropical garden as well as a vast expanse of lawn. Picnic facilities enhance the grounds of Fort Scaur.

P   Bermuda's biggest bird sanctuary, Spittal Pond, runs along the south coast in Smith's Parish. Lesser reserves of wild marshes and woods are situated in several other areas. Bird-lovers also find company in the giant trees of the Arboretum and the Botanical Gardens.

PETS. If you can't bear to leave Fido at home, be sure to check with the airline or shipping line about the problems and paperwork involved in traveling with a pet. And find out whether your hotel will accept animals.

PHOTOGRAPHY. Major brands of film are readily available in Bermuda, and same-day processing is advertised for all types of stock except Kodachrome, which takes longer.

Those brilliant skies and blinding white roofs make beautiful pictures, but you'll have to be careful to avoid over-exposure. In Bermuda, as in other sea resorts, the sand and salt air mean you have to protect your camera. And try to keep camera and film out of the hot sun. If you have any problems, there are competent repairmen to fix any camera that's stuck or broken. If the worst happens, you could hardly hope to find a better place to buy a new camera at a favorable price.

Some airport security machines use X-rays which can ruin your film. Ask that it be checked separately, or enclose it in a lead-lined bag.

POLICE. Bermuda's unarmed policemen, in their constable helmets and Bermuda shorts, are a tourist attraction in themselves. They are recruited in Britain and the West Indies as well as locally. You should address a policeman or policewoman as "officer". They're quite cordial about answering questions, giving directions and even posing for pictures.

PUBLIC HOLIDAYS

Movable dates:	Good Friday
	Queen's Birthday (mid-June)
	Cup Match and Somers Day (the Thursday and Friday before the first Monday in August; classic cricket match)

Jan. 1	New Year's Day
May 24	Bermuda Day (formerly observed as Commonwealth Day. Empire Day and Queen Victoria's Birthday)
Nov. 11	Remembrance Day (anniversary of Armistice ending World War I, honoring all war dead)
Dec. 25	Christmas Day
Dec. 26	Boxing Day (marking the old English custom of day-after-Christmas gift boxes for employees, apprentices, service personnel)

Note: Public holidays falling on a weekend are usually observed the following Monday, when businesses and most restaurants are closed.

RADIO and TV. Bermuda has three commercial television channels broadcasting in color from morning to night. Major U.S. television network morning and evening news programs are broadcast simultaneously on Bermuda television stations. There is a local cable television network carrying the same cable programs available in the U.S., and satellite television is also popular.

There are several commercial AM radio stations transmitting music, local newscasts, religious programs galore, and certain shows in Portuguese for Azorean immigrants. One carries British Broadcasting Corporation news and programs in the afternoons and evenings. Two FM stations specialize in uninterrupted music.

RELIGIOUS SERVICES. The capital. Hamilton, has two cathedrals —the stately Bermuda Cathedral (Anglican) on Church Street and St. Theresa's Cathedral (Roman Catholic), in Spanish colonial style, on Cedar Avenue. More than a dozen denominations are represented in Bermuda. For full details of services, see the Friday and Saturday editions of *The Royal Gazette.*

SHIPWRECKS. Scuba divers are welcome to explore Bermuda's well-known shipwreck sites, just for fun. They are referred to as un-protected wrecks. But divers interested in so-called protected wrecks, where treasure may be found, will encounter serious bureaucratic obstacles. Only divers specially licensed by the official grandly named the Receiver of Wreck are allowed to go down to protected wrecks, and those licenses are normally issued only to Bermudians.

S **SHOPPING HOURS.** Shops and stores are generally open Monday through Saturday from 9 or 9:15 a.m. to 5 or 5:30 p.m. Some stores reopen in the evenings and on Sundays, when cruise liners are in port. Shops in big hotels are often open later.

SIGHTSEEING HOURS. All churches and the cathedrals are open daily.

Aquarium (Museum and Zoo). 9 a.m.–5 p.m. daily except Christmas Day.

Art Gallery (Hamilton City Hall). 10:30 a.m.–4:30 p.m. Mon.–Fri., 9 a.m.–noon Sat.

Bermuda Historical Society Museum. 9:30 a.m.–4:30 p.m. (closes for lunch), closed Wed. and Sun.

Bermuda Library. 9:30 a.m.–6 p.m. Mon.–Fri., till 5 p.m. on Sat.

Bermuda Maritime Museum. 10 a.m.–5 p.m. daily (last admission 4:30 p.m.) except Christmas Day.

Botanical Gardens. Sunrise to sunset daily. Guided tours at 10:30 a.m. Tues., Wed. and Fri. from April to November; Tues. and Fri. only from December to March.

Cabinet Building. 9 a.m.–5 p.m. Mon.–Fri.

Camden House. Noon–2 p.m. Tues. and Fri.

Carriage Museum. 9 a.m.–4 p.m. Mon.–Sat., closed holidays.

Carter Historic House. 10 a.m.–2 p.m., Wed.

Coin Exhibition (Bank of Bermuda). 9:30 a.m.–3 p.m. Mon.–Fri.

Confederate Museum. 10 a.m.–5 p.m. Mon.–Sat.

Crystal Caves. 9 a.m.–5 p.m. daily (last admission 4:30 p.m.) except Christmas Day.

Deliverance. 10 a.m.–4 p.m. daily except Good Friday, Easter Sunday and Christmas Day.

Devil's Hole. 9:30 a.m.–4:30 p.m. Mon.–Sat., from 10 a.m. on Sun. and holidays, closed in January, on Good Friday and Christmas Day.

Featherbed Alley Print Shop. 10 a.m.–4 p.m. Mon.–Sat., closed on holidays.

Fort Hamilton. 9:30 a.m.–5 p.m. Mon.–Fri.

Fort St. Catherine. 10 a.m.–4 p.m. daily except Christmas Day.

Fort Scaur. 8 a.m.–4:30 p.m. daily except Christmas Day and Boxing Day.

Gates Fort. 9:30 a.m.–4:30 p.m. daily.

Gibb's Hill Lighthouse. 9 a.m.–4:30 p.m. daily except Christmas Day.

Hamilton City Hall. 9 a.m.–5 p.m. Mon.–Fri.

Leamington Caves. 9:30 a.m.–4:15 p.m. daily except Good Friday and Christmas Day.

N.A.S.A. To arrange for visits, tel. 293-1142.

Old Rectory. 10 a.m.–4 p.m. two days a week (check by calling 297-0879).

Old State House. 10 a.m.–4 p.m. Wed.

Palm Grove Garden and Aviary. 9 a.m.–4 p.m. Mon.–Thurs.

Perfume Factory. 9 a.m.–5 p.m. Mon.–Sat., 10 a.m.–4 p.m. Sun.

Perot Post Office. 8 a.m.–5 p.m. Mon.–Fri., till noon only on Sat.

President Henry Tucker House. 10 a.m.–5 p.m. Mon.–Sat.

St. George's Historical Society Museum. 10 a.m.–4 p.m. Mon.–Fri.

Sessions House. 9 a.m.–5 p.m. Mon.–Fri.

Somers Gardens. 7:30 a.m.–4:30 p.m. daily.

Springfield Library. 9 a.m.–5 p.m. Mon., Wed. and Sat., closed 1–2 p.m. for lunch.

Town Hall (St. George's). 9 a.m.–5 p.m. Mon.–Fri.

Verdmont. 10 a.m.–4 p.m. Mon.–Sat. (closed for lunch).

TAXES. Bermudians enjoy a society free from income tax, but governments always find a way... For instance, a 6% Hotel Occupancy Tax is added to every hotel bill, regardless of the meal plan involved, to be paid at checkout time. At the airport, departing passengers are slapped with a Passenger Tax. (Ships' passengers are charged a $15 Departure Tax, but this is collected in advance by the shipping companies.)

TIME DIFFERENCES. Bermuda is on Atlantic Standard Time, one hour ahead of Eastern Standard Time and four hours behind Greenwich Mean Time. From the end of April to the end of October Bermuda goes on Daylight Saving Time, so the difference with New York stays the same year-round.

Los Angeles	New York	**Bermuda**	London
8 a.m.	11 a.m.	**noon**	4 p.m.

T **TIPPING.** Many hotels and guest houses add 10%, or a fixed sum per person per day, to the bill as a service charge, relieving guests of any tipping problems. In many restaurants a 15% gratuity is added to the bill, in which case no further tip is expected (if not added, leave 10 to 15%). Hairdressers and barbers also expect 15%, as do taxi and carriage drivers. One departure from British tradition: in a Bermuda pub, the bartender will not be offended by a tip, and in fact expects one (15%). There's no need to tip porters, bellboys, maids or doormen except in case of exceptional service.

TOILETS. Although American euphemisms like "rest room" are often used, the wide availability of public conveniences reflects a British tradition. The most centrally located facility is alongside the Visitors Service Bureau in Hamilton. Many public parks and beaches have toilets, as well. And the facilities in hotels and restaurants keep to a high standard.

TOURIST INFORMATION OFFICES. The main office of the Bermuda Department of Tourism is in Global House, 43 Church Street, Hamilton 5–24, Bermuda.

Overseas regional offices:

Canada:	Suite 1004, 1200 Bay Street, Toronto, Ont. M5R 2A5
United Kingdom and Europe	BCB Ltd., 1 Battersea Church Road, London SW11 3LY
U.S.A.	Suite 2008, 235 Peachtree Street, N.E., Atlanta, GA 30303
	Suite 1010, 44 School Street, Boston, MA 02108
	Suite 1070, 150 North Wacker Drive, Chicago, IL 60606
	Suite 201, 310 Madison Avenue, New York, NY 10017

Once in Bermuda, you can pick up maps and leaflets at any of the Visitors Service Bureau offices at the airport, in Hamilton, St. George's and Somerset.

TRANSPORTATION

Buses*. Comfortable, modern pink-and-blue buses cover Bermuda from tip to tip, adhering to the timetables with an almost Swiss attention to punctuality. A free leaflet containing all the bus (and ferry) schedules includes a route map, full information on fares, and even a suggested bus-and-ferry sightseeing itinerary. Note that some lines operate only in the daytime, and weekend service is curtailed. Along the roads, bus stops are marked by poles painted in broad green and white stripes. You must deposit the exact fare in the box at the front entrance of the bus; drivers do not give change. If you plan to do a lot of traveling by bus, you can buy reduced-price ticket booklets at the central bus station in Hamilton or at post offices. According to picture-warnings posted in the buses, smoking and eating are prohibited.

Ferries*. Bermuda's small, peppy ferryboats criss-cross Hamilton Harbour, saving commuters the drive and offering tourists some low-budget sightseeing. From the deck you get a fine view of visiting cruise ships, freighters, yachts, and the landscape of Bermuda and its off-islands. There are ten embarkation points, the principal terminal being alongside the Visitors Service Bureau, Front Street, Hamilton. Be sure to have correct change for the turnstiles. Note that Sunday and holiday service is greatly reduced, and the "long-distance" route across the Great Sound is liable to cancellation in stormy weather.

Taxis*. All Bermuda taxis are clearly marked with a "Taxi" sign on the roof, illuminated when the cab is available for hire. There are taxi ranks at the airport and docks and at all the important hotels. Taxis, most of them radio-dispatched, may also be ordered by phone—at 295-4141, 292-5600, or 292-4476.

In addition to the metered fare, you are liable to a 25% surcharge between 10 p.m. and 6 a.m. and on Sundays and public holidays. There is also an extra charge for luggage carried on the roof or in the trunk (boot). No more than four passengers may travel together in some taxis, six in others.

Taxis may be engaged by the hour or day for sightseeing. Any taxi displaying a small blue flag is driven by a driver-guide with qualifications approved by the Department of Tourism.

Carriages*. For visitors in no hurry, the most romantic way to get around is in the splendor of one of Bermuda's horse-carriages. They come in various designs and sizes, covered or uncovered, one horse or two. Most of the surrey fleet is stationed along Front Street in Hamilton.

WATER. Mid-ocean rain is the source of Bermuda's delicious drinking water. It rolls down the furrows of those distinctive white Bermuda roofs and into underground tanks. You can drink it from the tap with pleasure and without a care. But don't waste this precious resource.

Index

An asterisk (*) next to a page number indicates a map reference. For index to Practical Information, see inside front cover.

INDEX